Arnt Cobbers

Architecture in Berlin

The 100 most Important Buildings
and Urban Settings

With Photographs by Günter Schneider

Jaron Verlag

Extended and updated edition
1st Printing of this edition 2011
© 1998–2011 Jaron Verlag GmbH, Berlin
(Original title: "Architekturführer. Die 100 wichtigsten
Berliner Bauwerke")

www.jaron-verlag.de
Translation: Victor Dewsbery, Berlin; Miriamne Fields, Berlin;
Marie Frohling, Berlin
Cover design: Bauer + Möhring, Berlin, using a photograph
by Günter Schneider (Jewish Museum / Libeskind Building)
Design and layout: Prill Partners I producing, Berlin
Lithography: LVD GmbH, Berlin
Printed and bound by: AZ Druck und Datentechnik GmbH, Berlin

ISBN 978-3-89773-415-9

List of Contents

Foreword

Berlin is not a simple city in terms of its architectural history. The substance of its buildings has frequently suffered – not only in the disastrous days of the Second World War. Throughout the 800 year history of the city, economic growth has often been associated with a new self-consciousness which demanded to find expression in architecture – to the detriment of the older, historically developed structures.

It is true that there were always strong adherents of monument conservation in Berlin – Schinkel can be regarded as one of the precursors of conservation in Germany – but Berlin has never been a model of respectful treatment of historical buildings. This has not changed even today; we only need to remind ourselves of the demolition of most of the old Hotel Esplanade at the same time as a copy of the old Hotel Adlon was being built opposite it. Or the demolition of the Lehrter Stadtbahnhof railway station, which had been admirably restored only ten years ago – although it was the only building far and wide, it was allegedly not possible to integrate it into the new central station.

However, if we keep our eyes open as we go through the city we can still discover surprising and wonderful structures. This book hopes to direct the reader's attention to overlooked or unnoticed buildings and to unveil qualities that are perhaps not apparent at first sight. But in order to develop a sense of the innovative and unconventional, it is necessary to place the buildings into their historical context; we need to know what went before them.

Logically, this book is chronologically structured as far as this is possible and rational. The names of the historical epochs are given as a guideline, even though the categories are not always clear, especially in 20th century architecture. For example, the architecture of National Socialism still does not have a generally accepted historical title, and the boundary between Modernism and Post-Modernism is still a subject of controversy.

Selecting 100 works of architecture is not an easy task for a city of this size. The choice must necessarily be subjective, but two historical considerations were prominent. On the one hand, the buildings had to be accessible for tourists. Interesting buildings which can only be viewed after a long journey of discovery had to be left out. On the other hand, a number of buildings in the central areas of Unter den Linden and the City West were included although, taken on their own, they would perhaps not be counted among the 100 most important buildings.

Moreover, the 100 works of architecture should provide an overview of the architectural history of Berlin from the 13th century to the present day. Two epochs are particularly well represented, and – without wishing to be unfair to many important individual works and their architects – they are the periods which secure the position of Berlin in the history of architecture: the Schinkel period and the 1920s.

Contemporary buildings from the last twenty years are also well represented. Here, however, only history will decide which architectural trends will establish themselves and have a lasting significance.

The Architectural History of Berlin

Berlin is older than it appears. In 1987, both the East and the West held 750th anniversary celebrations, but they merely commemorated the first mention of Berlin's sister town of Cölln. Berlin is certainly older than 800 years, but there are unfortunately hardly any documents from the early period of history. They were probably destroyed in the fires that ravaged the city.

After Brandenburg fortress was conquered in 1157 and the area between the rivers Elbe and Oder had finally come under German rule, the new rulers – the margraves and their knights – attracted colonists from the west of the Empire into the densely wooded and thinly populated expanses of land. Within about 150 years, a dense network of villages sprung up. These villages were all similar in structure, clustered along a road with a village green at the centre and a single stone building – the village church. Even today, a number of these granite village churches are still found in the districts of Berlin, and even the layout of the village green is often preserved, even where the building development no longer has any semblance of village life such as in Wilmersdorf and Schöneberg.

At the time, the river Spree with its marshy lowlands was a barrier which could only be crossed at very few points. In the area now covered by Berlin there were three fords, two of which were protected by fortresses: Köpenick and Spandau. German merchants settled near older Slavic settlements in both of these locations, and both were given town charters in the 13th century. But whereas Spandau flourished and became one of the most important towns in the region – with strong support from the margraves – Köpenick was never able to compete successfully with its vigorous neighbour Berlin.

Half way between Köpenick and Spandau, the valley of the Spree becomes narrower between the higher land of the Barnim to the north and the Teltow to the south. Here there were a number of sandy islands in the valley which facilitated river crossing and provided firm ground for building on. In the last decades of the 12th century, resting places for merchants arose on both banks, and they grew to become permanent settlements: Cölln to the south on an island of the Spree and Berlin to the north. Early on, a bridge was built, the "Mühlendamm", which held back the river Spree and enabled mills to be operated – and later enabled the river to be diverted into the protecting town moat. Whereas the town of Cölln was restricted to the southern part of the Spree island – the north was too marshy – the town of Berlin, which was already twice as large, had room to expand. The two towns retained their separate identity even into the 18th century, even though they had a joint town hall for part of this period on a bridge over the Spree, but they were often jointly referred to as just Berlin, the name under which they were finally unified in 1709.

Nothing remains of the old town of Cölln. The centre of the settlement was the fish market with St. Peter's church, the most recent version of which was built in the 19th century and demolished in 1963 after war damage. The second bridgehead, the Molkenmarkt, became the new centre of Berlin and nearby to the north the settlers erected their first church, St. Nikolai, dedicated to the patron saint of merchants.

The double town quickly developed, and its development was favoured by the busy route from the south and Magdeburg to Stettin, which crossed the Spree here. Merchants from Berlin soon entered into trade with Poland, the Baltic towns, Hamburg and even Flanders. From 1359 Berlin is documented as a member of the Hanseatic league. The economic boom made it possible to build three fine churches and one brick wall which was completed around 1320. A further structure which was first built in the second decade of the 13th century near to the Franciscan monastery was the "Hohes Haus", the town residence of the margraves who – like all mediaeval rulers – travelled the land from one fortress to the next. Berlin began to overtake the other two major towns in the region, Brandenburg / Havel (which was also once a double town) and the more recent Frankfurt / Oder. At the end of the 14th century, Berlin was at the head of the league of the towns of the Mittelmark.

The glorious era of the self-sufficient merchant town ended in the 15th century. After the town had been ruled by weak rulers for many years, Friedrich von Hohenzollern became the margrave of Brandenburg in 1415, a title which had since 1348 conferred the right to be one of the seven electors of the Empire (the body which elected the German king in the cathedral of Frankfurt / Main). From 1443 onwards he had a permanent castle built in the northern part of Cölln, and from 1470 it became the permanent residence of the Elector and the seat of the highest authorities and the courts – in face of bitter resistance from the citizens whose privileges were gradually whittled away by the Elector.

Berlin became a residence city and thus received new economic and cultural stimulus. Having been stricken by the plague several times and suffered greatly during the Thirty Years' War, it was finally developed as an attractive residence city in the baroque period under Friedrich Wilhelm the Great Elector (1640–88) who fortified the town, which then had about 6000 inhabitants, added the new settlements of Friedrichswerder (from 1662) and Doro-theenstadt (from 1668) and created the tree-lined boulevard Unter den Linden. In addition, the Edict of Potsdam of 1685 brought many Huguenots (Protestant religious refugees from France) to the city, and they had a profound effect on the city's economy and culture. In 1710, Berlin already had 56 000 inhabitants.

A new chapter in the architectural history of Berlin began with Friedrich III., who crowned himself as the king of Prussia (Friedrich I.) in Königsberg in 1701. With his new title he not only wished to have worthy ceremonies, he also wanted the architecture of the city to reflect his tastes – in fact, he began building splendid new buildings after his accession as Elector in 1688. Charlottenburg Palace, the Zeughaus and especially the splendid extension of the town palace (with the coin tower by Schlüter which unfortunately collapsed) were the first buildings of international renown in Ber-lin. Where Dutch architecture had been the great example in the previous decades (due to the Great Elector's family connections and personal preferences), Berlin architecture under the archi-tects Andreas Schlüter, Eosander von Göthe and Jean de Bodt now caught up with the international "standard" dictated by France and Italy. But Friedrich's demands almost ruined the state financially, so that his son Friedrich Wilhelm I., the soldier king, put an end to the rapid building programme and cut back the regal splendour to a minimum. Nevertheless, a building movement began in this era and lasted throughout the 18th century – and has left its mark on the city.

From 1734 onwards, the old fortifications were cleared away and a lower wall (to counter desertion by the many soldiers and to enforce customs duties) was built around a far larger urban area which can still be traced today by the names of streets and squares. Large areas within this wall were still undeveloped in the middle of the 19th century.

Under Friedrich II., known as the Great (1740–86), Prussia became a major European power and Berlin became a European metropolis in its architecture, its culture and its academic life. The leading architects of "Friedrich's baroque" were Knobelsdorff, Gontard, Unger and the Boumann family. This epoch was marked by its elegant and sometimes classically strict facades, whereas the flamboyant forms of the (French-inspired) rococo were dominant in its interior architecture.

After the death of Friedrich the Great in 1786, much later than in the rest of Europe, classicism became established in the city that was later known as "Athens on the Spree". Antiquity, and particularly ancient Greek art, now became the standard. The most famous example is the Brandenburg Gate, which Carl Gotthard Langhans designed to copy the propylaeum in Athens. The rise of Berlin architecture after the years of the Napoleonic occupation was linked with the name of Karl Friedrich Schinkel, whose buildings are characterised by clear cubic forms, balanced proportions and their reference to models from antiquity. For more than half a century, Schinkel and his pupils had a dominant influence on the appearance of the city.

It was only with the establishment of the unified German Reich in 1871 that a new epoch began: Historicism, which ironically came from France, the nation that Germany had just defeated, and which dominated architecture in Berlin for about 40 years. The sober, "disciplined" classical style now gave way to a "loud", extravagant style which unashamedly borrowed Renaissance and baroque forms. This gave rise to wildly dynamic facades that were often far too elaborate.

In the course of the 18th century, Berlin had already become a major city for the crafts, and during the 19th century it became the largest industrial city in Germany and one of the largest cities in Europe with 265 000 inhabitants in 1834, growing to 826 000 in 1871, 966 000 in 1875 and 2 040 100 in 1905.

Great industrial areas arose around the imperial capital, and as a result of the general zoning plan developed by James Hobrecht in 1858–61 (authorised by the state rather than the city, and thus extending beyond the boundaries of Berlin), large residential districts for the workers were built, making Berlin the largest city of barrack-style accommodation in the world.

The wealthy moved out, especially to the neighbouring communities to the west. Berlin itself was weighed down by the social burdens that resulted from the high proportion of proletarians. That only changed in 1920, when a major administrative breakthrough was achieved after many years of tenacious debate: out of eight towns, 59 rural communities and 27 estates, the city of greater Berlin was formed with an area of 880 square kilometres and over four million inhabitants, thus making it the largest city in Europe at the time.

Historicism passed its peak around the turn of the century, and more and more architects looked for a new formal language in keeping with the changing times. After the end of the First World War, Berlin became a centre of Modernism, although its development was impeded by the economic crisis around 1930 and interrupted by the seizure of power by the National Socialists.

The 1920s saw the development of the infrastructure (airport, harbours) and the construction of residential estates, and the years after 1933 were marked by monumental National Socialist buildings and the monstrous town planning designs for the "world capital city of Germania", which were fortunately not put into practice. The demolition programme which the National Socialists did not achieve by "peaceful" means was accomplished by the Second World War which they had started: large areas of the city were destroyed in the air raids and street fighting which lasted until the very last days of the war because Berlin was declared to be a "fortress" which must be defended to the last man. 32 per cent of the dwellings and 20 per cent of the buildings in Berlin were destroyed – in the district of Berlin-Mitte it was as much as 54 per cent of the dwellings. But destruction of the traditional building substance in Berlin was even more extensive during the "redevelopment" from the 1950s to the 1970s.

As a result of the treaty between the Allies, the capital of the German Reich was divided into four sectors, and by 1949 these had developed into "Berlin (West)" and "Berlin, capital of the GDR". The eastern part of the city had 45.6 per cent of the land and (in 1945) 37 per cent of the population.

The division of the city was of course also reflected in its architecture. Both halves of the city became showcases for their respective social systems, and after the Wall was built in 1961, planning in each part of the city no longer took any account of the other half.

The city has now been reunited since 1990, and the common architectural development in the whole of Berlin has only been in existence for two decades. The politicians, who set the framework, were faced with the daunting task of forming a unity out of two disparately developed halves, closing up the wasteland, but without completely erasing the traces of history or smoothing over the contrasts. This is a fascinating task for urban planners and architects, but in view of the indecision of many official bodies in the city it is also often a frustrating task.

The largest undeveloped areas have by now been built on and the important building projects have been completed. Others – like the areas around the Central Train Station and the former East Harbour – are still under construction or even in the planning stages. It is still too soon to make a final judgment on the quality of the architecture and city planning. But one thing is certain: Virtually no other city has such a wide range of high-quality modern structures as does Berlin.

The Buildings

St. Nikolaikirche (St. Nicholas Church, Mitte)

The Nikolaikirche, which is dedicated to the patron saint of merchants, was the first and most important parish church in mediaeval Berlin. The first stone building, which probably arose around 1230, was a pillar basilica of field stone (model in the church). The only surviving part is the four-storey lower section of the western tower, an almost fortress-like structure.

At the end of the 13th century, the nave became a brick-built hall-type church with three aisles of equal height, a spatial form which occurred in the area without any predecessors, and within a few years became the dominant architectural style of town parish churches in Brandenburg. The present ambulatory was begun in the 1370s, but building work was interrupted by the town fire of 1380. It is not clear when the chancel was completed, but it was probably later than 1400. The present nave, the northern chancel extension and the chapel of Our Lady in the south-west were built in the middle of the 15th century.

The chancel and ambulatory are no longer concentrically arranged like in a classical cathedral, instead they create a spatial perspective. The sub-division into so many wall sections is unusual for Brandenburg and indicates a high level of prestige, as do the zigzag and rope-like (twisted) bars in the interior. The two polygons are linked by so-called jumping vaults.

Outside the building appears compact, especially because of its large roof. In the inside, the outer wall is varied and transparent in its structure as a result of the chapel section, the gallery and the recessed wall surfaces. A clear transition can be seen where the chancel meets the nave, and up close it becomes apparent that the nave and chancel are different in structure both inside and outside. In the 15th century there were plans for a double tower front, but only the southern tower with a octagonal spire was built, and the north tower ended in a gable with a ridge roof.

The present symmetrical structure with the two polygon towers

is the work of Hermann Blankenstein in 1876–78. After heavy damage during the war, the church was restored in 1980–87 for the 750th anniversary celebrations in Berlin. The original colour was recreated from the few remaining remnants of the vaults. The church is now used as a sacred museum.

Gothic
Tower base around 1230; chancel around 1380; nave around 1460; double tower front 1876–78
Mitte, Nikolaiviertel
Open: daily 10–18 hrs., Tel. 24 00 21 62
www.stadtmuseum.de
▷ S / U Alexanderplatz, U Klosterstrasse, bus 100

St. Marienkirche (St. Mary's Church)

The Marienkirche was built as the parish church of the new town of the time. It is not known when this extension of the town with its regular street grid was built – perhaps it was when the town charter was granted around 1230, or perhaps it was later. The building dates for the Marienkirche are also unknown. It must have been in use by 1294. It is known that it was damaged by one of the great town fires of 1376 and 1380, and it was perhaps reconstructed in an altered form. But the architecture clearly dates from the 13th century and is fundamentally different from the more recent architecture of the Nikolaikirche.

A characteristic feature is the elongated structure of the building. The wide dividing arches create a clear separation of the three aisles, but the wide arcades of the side aisles make the spatial appearance wider, so that there is not the noticeable uniform height that is typical of classical cathedrals. The chancel has a single aisle and only appears lower from the outside due to the roof.

The spatial form is taken from churches of the beggars' orders. Dominicans and Franciscans were extremely successful at the time, and their architecture influenced the architecture of many town parish churches. The characteristic form of the chalice-shaped grouped columns, which was later also used in the Nikolaikirche, was based on the Franciscan church (Klosterstrasse) which was unfortunately destroyed in the war and is now just a ruin, and it was also reminiscent of the groups of columns in classical cathedrals.

The oblique support columns in the western part of the exterior show that the western part, which gives the appearance of being part of the original structure and is made of erratic stone blocks, is actually more recent. The tower dates from the 15th century and the present copper top section, which is a mixture of baroque and neo-Gothic stylistic elements, was designed by Carl Gotthard Langhans, the architect of the Brandenburg Gate (1789 / 90). The southern aspect with the four equal gables, which integrates the

14th century sacristy, was added in 1893 by Hermann Blankenstein.

The highlights in the interior include the impressive pulpit by
Andreas Schlüter (1702 / 03), the organ of 1720–23 (prospect by
Johann Georg Glume) and especially the fresco "Dance of Death" in
the tower hall, which was probably created after the plague of 1484.

Near the church, at Spandauer Strasse 1–2a, is a further mediaeval building, the former chapel of the Heiliggeist-Spital (Holy Spirit hospital), which was first mentioned in 1313 and has a star-ribbed
vault dating from 1476. It was integrated into the building of a
business college in 1905 / 06 and when the renovation is complete
will be used as a banquet hall by the Institute of Economics of the
Humboldt University.

Gothic
13th & 14th century with later additions
Mitte, Karl-Liebknecht-Strasse 8
Open: daily 10–18 hrs., Tel. 242 44 67
www.marienkirche-berlin.de
▷ S / U Alexanderplatz, bus 100

St. Nikolaikirche
(St. Nicholas Church, Spandau)

To experience the flair of an old town setting in Berlin, you must travel out to Spandau. Not only the mediaeval street pattern is preserved here, the old buildings and the small town atmosphere are also preserved – although this atmosphere is marred by large modern buildings such as the Karstadt department store.

Spandau is older than Berlin. There was probably a fortified Slavic embankment to the south of the present old town as early as the 10th century, and to the north the Ascanian fortress – the citadel of today – was built on an island in the 12th century. With the protection of the citadel and the favourable location at the junction of the rivers Spree and Havel, a merchants' settlement arose at the end of the 12th century and was granted its town charter in 1232.

The Nikolaikirche was the parish church of this wealthy merchant town and the seat of the provost. No records of the building process have survived, but dendrochronological studies have shown that the timber used for the roof was felled in the winter of 1368 / 69. It is known that timber was used for construction soon after it was felled in the Middle Ages, so the whole building must probably be dated to the 1360s. The transition from the chancel columns to the vault leads us to assume that a different vault was probably planned originally, but on the whole the church appears very coherent in its style.

Thus it appears to be one of the very oldest hall-type churches with an ambulatory. The design is similar to the Nikolaikirche in Berlin. Here, too, the inner chancel and outer wall are not concentrically arranged as in the high Gothic style. The external wall is sub-divided into seven sides of a fourteen-sided polygon, but the inner chancel only has three subdivisions. Alternating four-part and three-part vaults link the two polygons.

With four nave pillars, the Nikolaikirche in Spandau is considerably shorter than its Berlin counterpart and its individual forms

are simpler (for example, the Berlin church has an inner wall with chapels and a gallery and the intricate grouped pillars with their zigzag patterns). The chancel and nave in Spandau are uniform in their design, and the short chancel is skilfully extended in its spatial impact by two symmetrically added two-storey side chapels. Thus, the church as a whole is more balanced in its proportions and creates a composed spatial atmosphere.

The solid western spire was built in 1467 / 68, and its top was once higher than all other spires in the Brandenburg region. The present baroque upper section dates from 1740–44, and the gothic-style surface arcades were added by Schinkel. The church was severely damaged in the Second World War and restored by 1958, but without the baroque balconies.

Gothic
1360s; spire 1467–68; top section of spire 1740–44
Spandau, Reformationsplatz 1
Open: Mon–Fri 12–16 hrs., Sat 11–15 hrs., Sun 14–16 hrs.; Tel. 333 56 39
www.nikolai-spandau.de
▷ U Altstadt Spandau

Dorfkirche Dahlem (Dahlem Village Church)

The city boundaries of Berlin enclose a large number of former villages, all of which were founded in the colonisation phase up to about 1300. Almost all were built around a village green, and this design can still often be seen in the street layout. The only buildings that survive from the Middle Ages are the old village churches, over 20 of which are still preserved, although some have been altered and extended – often larger window openings were made in the walls and new towers or spires were added. (The oldest and only remaining example of a "classical" 13th century village church is the church in Marienfelde, almost on the southern edge of the city. It is the only church to show the archetypal interplay of four different elements: a broad rectangular southern tower with a ridge roof, a rectangular nave, a narrower and lower square chancel and an even lower, semicircular apse).

The most elaborate village church after extensions, which is frequently visited due to its proximity to the Domäne Dahlem and the Dahlem museum complex, is the Annenkirche (St. Anne's church), which is untypically close to the crossing point of two old main roads and is surrounded by a cemetery. The brick building on a field stone pedestal was built in several phases. The foundations, and possibly the lower parts of the single-aisle nave, probably date from the 13th century. Two windows on the northern side and a bricked-in window on the south have Romanesque round arches, but a bricked-in south portal has pointed arches.

In the 15th century the polygonal, vaulted chancel was added. Its floor plan and the four large windows with their simple tracery typical of the time show the influence of "great" architecture, especially the urban parish churches of Berlin and Spandau, on the design of village churches. It was probably at the same time that the burial chapel with its decorative half-timbered gable was built, which is now the sacristy.

The church was severely damaged in the Thirty Years' War, and the nave structure was probably built higher after the war – the line of plaster probably marks the top of the old wall. The two large windows to the south of the nave date from this period, and the previously flat-roofed nave was vaulted. The wooden tower dates from 1781, and the spire at the top from 1953. From 1832–49 the tower served as a relay station in the telegraph line from Berlin to Koblenz.

At the end of the 19th century, a number of old frescos were discovered on the walls of the nave, and most of them have now been expertly restored. They show scenes from the Passion of Christ and of St. Anna, who is also at the centre of the fine carved altar dating from the 16th century.

Gothic
13th century; chancel 15th century; altered several times
Dahlem, corner of Königin-Luise-Strasse and Pacelliallee
Open: Sat / Sun 11–13 hrs., Tel. 841 70 50
www.kg-dahlem.de
▷ U Dahlem Dorf

Jagdschloss Grunewald
(Grunewald Hunting Palace)

Grunewald hunting palace is the oldest surviving palace building in the city of Berlin. Of the first city palace, which was built of brick from 1443–51, only a round tower by the river Spree, the "Grüner Hut" survived, and that was demolished in 1950. And the major Renaissance palace which was built from about 1540 under Elector Joachim II. has also been lost without trace.

The hunting palace "Zum grünen Wald" (to the green forest), which gave the former Spandau Forest its name, is the best preserved of a whole series of hunting lodges which the Elector had built in the forests around the residence city. Once it was directly next to Grunewaldsee lake, but the water level has sunk dramatically. In 1709 a moat was built, making it a water palace.

The architect was probably Caspar Theiss, the architect of the "Stadtschloss" (city palace). But the present exterior appearance is mainly characterised by the baroque alterations to the complex under Johann Arnold Nering and Martin Grünberg (1669–1709).

The palace building, which is framed by low domestic outbuildings on three sides, consists of three storeys with a rectangular floor plan. Facing the courtyard, a polygonal staircase tower protrudes partly from the building – a typical Renaissance stylistic element. In front of this tower is a two-storey portal structure with a Renaissance decor marked with the date 1542, which formerly served as one end of the drawbridge over the moat. On the side facing the lake, the core building is framed by two tower-type wings with bays. The plain building has a white plaster facade with a belt-type facade around the ground floor. The mansard roof dates from the time of the baroque alterations. The Renaissance palace probably had gables and the windows were probably smaller and framed in sandstone similar to the windows that still survive in the portal structure.

The most interesting of the domestic outbuildings is the kitchen with its high gable next to the gateway. It originally had a flat roof, but a ribbed vault was added later.

The palace contains Berlin's only surviving Renaissance hall with its painted cassette-type ceiling, which was only rediscovered in 1973 during renovation work. The other rooms have plain baroque stucco ceilings.

Grunewald palace was used by the royal family until 1918, especially after the reintroduction of course hunting in Prussia in 1832, but the alterations from the 19th century were reversed to their former state after the war. In 1932 the palace became a paintings gallery with pictures from the former royal palaces, and because of the relatively small amount of war damage it was the first museum to reopen in Berlin in 1949.

Renaissance
Caspar Theiss around 1542; alterations by Johann Arnold Nering,
Martin Grünberg 1669–1709
Dahlem, Hüttenweg 100 (am Grunewaldsee)
Open: April–Oct Tues-Sun 10–18 hrs., Nov–March Sat, Sun & holidays
only by guided tours at 11, 13, 15 hrs., Tel. 813 35 97
www.spsg.de
▷ S Grunewald, bus 115, X10, X83 with a long walk

Zitadelle Spandau (Spandau Citadel)

In spite of damage and additions, the Spandau citadel is one of the best preserved Renaissance fortresses in Germany and still gives us an impression of how people in the 16th century tried to defend themselves against enemies.

The oldest parts of the fortifications date from the Middle Ages, and the Juliusturm tower, which is the emblem of Spandau, dates from the early 13th century and may be the oldest masonry structure in the city – and is certainly the oldest secular building.

Even in Slavic times, the point where the rivers Spree and Havel met was a place of great military importance, especially because it was possible to cross the Spree here. Archaeologists have excavated remains of a Slavic fortress which was replaced by a stone fortress in the 12th century after the Ascanians came to power. A "Protector Eberhard of Spandau" was first mentioned in 1197. The margraves often stayed in the Spandau fortress and staunchly supported the development of the nearby merchants' settlement.

The Juliusturm tower, named after Julius von Braunschweig-Wolfenbüttel, served as a keep and last place of refuge; the battlements were added by Schinkel. For many years the tower served as a dungeon and until 1918 the "Reich war treasure", consisting of reparation payments by France after the war of 1870 / 71, were kept under close guard here. The adjoining palace, the actual residential building, dates from the 15th century.

The decision to modernise the fortress in accordance with contemporary knowledge of fortress construction was made at the regional council meeting in Spandau in 1559. The Elector justified it with the need to protect the citizens of Spandau and his courtly state in nearby Berlin. The plans were by Francesco Chiaramella de Gandino, and the first construction supervisor was Christoph Römer before the Italian himself took over the work. The building was completed in 1594 under Count Rochus zu Lynar.

The citadel has a square pattern surrounded by a moat with

four bastions known as "König", "Kronprinz", "Brandenburg" and "Königin" at the corners (clockwise from the entrance).

The facade of the gatehouse, which contained the commander's residence above the portal, dates from 1839; only the sandstone gable is older. An impression of the original appearance can be gained from the courtyard side.

The barracks on the northern side and the magazine buildings in the east were added in the 19th century, and in the 1930s the buildings of the "army gas protection laboratories" were built, in which 300 people worked on the development of chemical weapons.

Today the citadel is used for cultural purposes – and as winter quarters for 10 000 bats.

Renaissance
Juliusturm tower and palace: 13th and 15th century; fortifications: Francesco Chiaramella de Gandino, Christoph Römer, Rochus Graf zu Lynar 1560–94; later alterations
Spandau, Am Juliusturm
Open: daily 10–17 hrs., Tel. 354 94 40
www.zitadelle-spandau.de
▷ U Zitadelle Spandau

Ribbeckhaus (Ribbeck House)

The Ribbeck house is the oldest residential building in the city and the only surviving Renaissance building in Berlin. It is all that remains of the old Berlin town hall which once stood in the present location of the Red Town Hall.

The Ribbeck house was built two years before Brandenburg was drawn into the Thirty Years' War which was so devastating for the region and its capital city. According to the inscription above the portal, it was built in 1624 by the privy councillor Hans Georg von Ribbeck and his wife Katharina von Brösicke by combining two older gable-fronted buildings and making them into an eaves-fronted building. Only four years later it was bought and altered by Duchess Anna Sophia von Braunschweig-Lüneburg, the daughter of Elector Johann Sigismund. After her death in 1659 it was used by the neighbouring riding stables, and later by the royal accounting chamber.

It requires imagination to envisage the original appearance of the building because an extra storey was added during alterations from 1803 / 04 which contrasts with the lower storeys in that it has groups of three windows. By royal command, the Renaissance gable roof which was removed for the alteration work was added again on top of the new storey. After damage in the war, the facade was restored in a simplified form. The richly sculptured portal shows ornamentation that is typical of the period, so-called gnarled ornamentation, and in the gable it contains the coat of arms of the Ribbeck family who built the house, held by angels.

The interior of the building is completely modern and its users include the Berlin department of the city library, who also use the neighbouring "Alter Marstall" (old riding stables), which is the only surviving building from the period of the baroque extension of the city and was built in 1665–70 by Michael Matthias Smids. This building, which was formerly used as accommodation for the Electoral / royal horses and coaches, housed the first Berlin court theatre from 1699–1713. To the left is the "Neuer Marstall" (new

riding stables, built in 1896–1902 by Ernst Ihne) which based its forms on the "Stadtschloss" (city palace) and presented a monumental facade towards the Spree. To the right of the Ribbeck house is the (former East Berlin) city library of 1964–65, which has an interesting portal by Fritz Kühn which shows the letter A in 117 different variations. Next to that is a neo-baroque building of the federal state archive and, on the corner of Mühlendamm, an office building designed by the Hamburg architectural office of Schweger und Partner and completed in 1999, which is the new headquarters of the major business associations in Germany: the German Industrial and Trade Association (DIHT), the Federal Association of German Industry (BDI) and the Federal Union of German Employers Associations (BDA).

Renaissance
1624, extended upwards 1803 / 04, facade simplified
Mitte, Breite Strasse 35
Open: Mon–Fri 10–20 hrs., Sat 10–19 hrs., Tel. 90 22 60
www.zlb.de
▷ U Spittelmarkt

Palais Schwerin (Schwerin Palace)

After the devastation in Berlin and Brandenburg caused by the Thirty Years' War and a series of epidemics, economic and cultural reconstruction only began gradually. The population was reduced by about half; of about 1200 houses before the war, only 750 were still inhabited in 1648. As early as 1641, Berlin was given building regulations by the new Elector Friedrich Wilhelm, the later Great Elector, which remained in force until 1853 and had long-term effects on the building style in the city. Thus, buildings with eaves facing the street replaced the gable-fronted buildings, and the custom of building around the rear courtyards developed from the middle of the 18th century.

Nothing remains of the fortifications built in 1658–83 under the direction of the Dutchman Johan Gregor Memhardt nor of the original buildings of the three planned extensions to the city. The oldest surviving town residences date from the period when Berlin was already being developed as a splendid residence city under the first Prussian king Friedrich I. Two examples of these buildings are the town residences of two state ministers: Palais Podewils in Klosterstrasse and Palais Schwerin on Molkenmarkt.

The latter was built for the state minister Otto von Schwerin from 1698–1704, probably as an alteration of two older buildings, to plans by Jean de Bodt. In 1937 it was moved back several metres and connected with the newly-built "Münze", which is decorated with a frieze created by Gottfried Schadow for the old "Münze" building which was pulled down in 1886.

Schwerin palace is a three-storey plaster-faced building. The central projection – unusually – has two balconies. This was intended to neutralise the fact that the entrance was originally arranged asymmetrically under the right-hand balcony, which was probably due to the layout of the previous buildings. The interior still has an elaborate staircase dating from the period of construction.

The building has been state-owned since 1766, and in 1794 it

became the property of the city government and was used as a criminal court and police headquarters. After the new police headquarters was built on Alexanderplatz, it was converted for residential use. Until 1990, it housed the Ministry of Culture of the GDR.

The nearby Podewils Palace on Klosterstrasse was also designed by Jean de Bodt and dates from 1701–04; the interior was altered in 1732 under State Minister von Podewils, a successor of Schwerin. The interior is modern; today the publically funded organization, "Kulturprojekte Berlin GmbH", has its headquarters here. The event hall has been used by the Grips Theatre as a second venue since 2009.

Baroque
Jean de Bodt 1698–1704; later altered
Mitte, Molkenmarkt 1–3
▷ U Klosterstrasse, S / U Alexanderplatz

Schloss Köpenick (Köpenick Palace)

Long before Berlin was fortified, the Ascanian fortress of Köpenick on the island of the Dahme had lost its strategic function. Under Elector Joachim II. it was converted to a hunting palace.

Electoral Prince Friedrich, who later became the first king of Prussia, had the building demolished and rebuilt from 1677 by Rutger van Langerfeld. His father, the Great Elector, spent many years of his youth in Holland, and his marriage to the Orange princess Luise Henriette strengthened the cultural links between the two states. As a result numerous Dutch architects came to Berlin in the decades after the Thirty Years' War, although few had more than moderate talent.

Köpenick palace was originally planned as a three wing building, but only the western wing was completed by 1681 (the foundations of the central wing were excavated). The southern section, which is plain and without sub-divisions on the side facing the courtyard, gives an idea of the plans for further construction. The solid frontage facing the water is sub-divided with projecting sections of three window axes in the centre and five on each side. The central projection is accentuated by various ornaments. The court facade is similarly structured.

The interior is symmetrical in design, and with its early baroque stucco decorations it appears heavy and ceremonious.

Of greater artistic significance is the palace chapel designed by Johann Arnold Nering, the major architect in Berlin after the death of Memhardt. The building was erected in 1684 / 85 and is three window axes wide, the same in depth and with an adjoining chancel with its walls forming three sides of a polygon. The facade, which rises above the simple domestic outbuildings on both sides (corresponding to the palace) is decorated with an Ionic pilaster arrangement which integrates the attic facade and culminates in sandstone figures of the four Evangelists, Moses and Melchizedek. The cupola is crowned by a lantern. The interior wooden barrel arch

vault is richly ornamented, but in a strictly classical style. Focal points are the richly carved pulpit and, above it, the wooden bust of Electoral Princess Elisabeth Henriette, the first wife of Friedrich III. who died early.

The two-storey gallery extension on the northern side of the palace courtyard (1688) was also designed by Nering. The round arches originally spanned large windows.

After Friedrich moved to the "Stadtschloss" (city palace) in 1688, Köpenick palace was only sporadically used and became a widow's home, a teaching college, a students' residence and, in 1963, the art and craft museum. Since 2004, following ten years of renovation work, the museum has presented an exhibition on spatial art.

Baroque
Rutger van Langerfeld 1677–81; chapel: Johann Arnold Nering 1684 / 85; gallery: Johann Arnold Nering 1688
Köpenick, Schloßinsel 1
Open: Tues–Sun 10–18 hrs., Tel. 657 15 04
www.smb.museum
▷ Tram 27, 60, 61, 62, 67, 68, bus 164, 167

Schloss Friedrichsfelde
(Friedrichsfelde Palace)

When the Elector of Brandenburg became the king of Prussia, this not only led to the architectural development of the residence city, at the centre of which was the magnificent extension of the palace by Andreas Schlüter and Eosander von Göthe. The area around Berlin also became a real residence region in which the king and his entourage restlessly moved from palace to palace. In addition to the older buildings in Köpenick, Potsdam ("Stadtschloss", town palace) and Oranienburg, there were now also the new buildings in Niederschönhausen (by Nering and Eosander), the palaces of Rosenthal and Blankenfelde which no longer survive and, as the most splendid building, Charlottenburg palace.

Friedrichsfelde palace, another impressive baroque building, was built in 1695 as a country house for the director general of the Electoral navy, Benjamin Raulé, probably to plans by Johann Arnold Nering. After the downfall of Raulé (who spent three years imprisoned in the Juliusturm tower in Spandau), the palace fell to the Elector who in 1717 gave it to Albrecht Friedrich from the removed family line of the margraves of Brandenburg-Schwedt. The new owner had it enlarged and more splendidly appointed by Martin Böhme, Eosander's successor as the palace architect in Berlin.

The original building had only five window axes, with a projected central axis and with a balcony, outdoor steps and a triangular gable. In 1719 the palace was extended by the addition of three axes on each side. The core building, which thus became the central projection, was crowned on both sides by a large gable. The present triangular gables and the form of the mansard roof are, in fact, alterations dating from the early 19th century. The palace saw frequent changes of ownership; it belonged to the youngest brother of Friedrich the Great, Prince Ferdinand, later to Duke Peter von Kurland who had the interior rooms redesigned in the classical style, and from 1816–1945 it belonged to the von

Treskow family. After the Second World War it was neglected for many years before the foundations were underpinned in the 1970s and restoration was completed in 1981. Little remains of the old interior, but the building still has the richly carved staircase and the stucco festival hall of 1785. The remaining rooms were decorated in keeping with the style with fittings from other palaces and estate houses.

The extensive palace park, which was designed as a landscape garden by Peter Josef Lenné in 1821, has been the home of the (East Berlin) zoo since 1955.

Baroque
Core building: probably by Johann Arnold Nering 1695; extension:
Martin Böhme 1719; alterations in the 19th century
Friedrichsfelde, Am Tierpark 125
Guided tours: Tues–Sun at 11, 12, 13, 14 hrs., Tel. 66 63 50 35
www.stadtmuseum.de
▷ U Tierpark

Schloss Charlottenburg
(Charlottenburg Palace)

The present complex is a combination of different building phases. The "Lustschloss Lietzenburg" (Lietzenburg pleasure palace) was built in 1695–99 to plans by Johann Arnold Nering for Electoress Sophie Charlotte, and the palace was renamed in her honour after her death in 1705. This oldest part comprises the present middle section. The middle of the side facing the gardens is accentuated by an oval room, which was probably intended to have a dome. From 1701, the palace was extended by the Paris-trained Swedish architect Johann Eosander von Göthe to a magnificent ensemble. On both sides, lower wings were added, forming a monumental facade on the garden side. On the side facing the city, two symmetrical narrow wings form a court of honour which is completed by railings. Eosander crowned the ensemble by adding a high tower with a dome and lantern above which Fortuna, the gold-plated goddess of happiness, can be seen.

To the west is the Orangerie with a length of 143 metres, which was completed in 1713. Work was only resumed in 1740 under Friedrich the Great. Originally, a second Orangerie had been planned, but instead of that the plain two-storey "new wing", with ornaments in the Friedrich rococo style, was built to plans by Knobelsdorff, who created a thematic link with the wall structure of the main building by designing a band-type facade.

The "Schlosstheater" (palace theatre), built in 1787–91 to plans by Carl Gotthard Langhans, was the last element of the building complex, added as an extension of the Orangerie. Today the building has a completely re-designed interior and houses up to 2009 the Museum of Pre and Early History. Its future use is unclear.

Behind the palace are the extensive gardens, with the front section in baroque symmetry and the far larger rear section as a landscape garden. Noteworthy features are the mausoleum of Queen Luise (1810–12 by Heinrich Gentz), the Belvedere (tea house, 1788, also designed by Langhans, now a porcelain museum) and the Schin-

kel pavilion which was built in 1824 / 25 as a summer house for King Friedrich Wilhelm II. The small Orangerie in front of the palace was designed by Georg Friedrich Boumann (1790).

The palace was severely damaged in the Second World War. It has been completely restored and houses a museum today.

The two buildings with high roof structures on the other side of Spandauer Damm, which were originally built as barracks (1851–59 by August Stüler), now house the Berggruen Museum (20th century art) and the Scharf-Gerstenberg Collection (Surrealists and their precursors).

Baroque
Main section: 1695–99 by Johann Arnold Nering and Martin Grünberg; extension by Eosander von Göthe 1701–13; new wing: Georg Wenzeslaus von Knobelsdorff 1740–46; theatre: Carl Gotthard Langhans 1787–91
Charlottenburg, Spandauer Damm 10–22
Open: main building: Tues–Sun 10–17 hrs., Knobelsdorff wing: Wed–Mon 10–17 hrs., Tel. 32 09 11
www.spsg.de
▷ Bus 109, 309

Zeughaus (Armoury)

The Zeughaus is the oldest building on Unter den Linden – and probably the finest building, too. Construction began in 1695 under the direction of Johann Arnold Nering, and after his death, work was continued by Martin Grünberg, Andreas Schlüter and, from 1699, Jean de Bodt. According to the inscription on the main portal, work was completed in 1706. Schlüter created the over 100 apex stones and the 22 impressive statues of dying warriors in the inner courtyard.

The building was originally built as a weapons armoury, and in 1877–81 the interior was redesigned as the hall of fame for Prussia and Brandenburg and a military museum. After heavy war damage, the building was restored until 1967 and used in the GDR period as a museum of German history. Since 1991 it has housed the German History Museum.

The four facades of the two-storey building, which is grouped around a square inner courtyard, are almost identical in their design, except that the portal facing Unter den Linden is more elaborate. The ground floor, with its round arch windows reaching down almost to ground level, gives the appearance of a solid field stone pedestal because of the colouring and the rustic (grooved) facade finish, but the building is actually made of bricks. The upper storey is highlighted by pilasters, window balustrades and the groups of figures above the windows. The subtle projections and recesses of the wall facade and the alternating window heads give rhythm to the long facades, and the middle is emphasised by the projection with the free-standing Tuscan pillars. The broken attic facade makes the roof line appear less heavy, and the building is crowned by trophies. The figures on the exterior celebrate victory, but the inner courtyard shows the other side of war, the death pangs of dying soldiers.

From 1998 to 2003 a new extension was added to the rear of the building and the inner courtyard was fitted with a glass roof to

plans by Ieoh Ming Pei. The museum was completely renovated, but the original room layout from the period of its reconstruction in the 1950s and 1960s has been preserved.

Andreas Schlüter, the brilliant sculptor, was not very lucky as an architect in Berlin. Because of inadequate building work, part of the rear facade collapsed on 5th august 1699. Schlüter had to surrender the construction supervision to Jean de Bodt, but he was nevertheless appointed as the chief palace architect. In this capacity he designed the monumental palace extension which was crowned by the "Münzturm" (coin tower). When this tower also collapsed – due to inadequate foundations – Schlüter was again dismissed and went to St. Petersburg, where he died a few years later.

Baroque
Johann Arnold Nering, Martin Grünberg, Andreas Schlüter, Jean de Bodt
1695–1706
Mitte, Unter den Linden 2
Open: daily 10–18 hrs., Tel. 20 30 44 44
www.dhm.de
▷ S / U Friedrichstrasse, U Französische Strasse, bus 100

Parochialkirche (Parochial Church)

After the Second Reformation under Elector Johann Sigismund failed in 1612, the Reformed church members in Brandenburg remained a small minority – including the ruling family and a number of the people at the court. In Berlin, Reformed church services were only held in the cathedral church which was attached to the palace, so the church members wanted to have a new church which would be independent of the court. In 1694, Friedrich III. approved the purchase of a plot of land, and the foundation stone was laid in 1695 with great pomp and in the presence of the Elector and the entire court. The architect was no lesser person than the head of the entire building programme in Brandenburg, chief architect Nering.

He designed a square central form with four adjoining semi-circular apse-like structures. On the side facing the street, a gable structure aimed to create an impressive entrance section. Nering died in 1695, and after the vault had collapsed, his successor Martin Grünberg simplified the plan and, instead of a ridge turret above the crossing point of the nave and transepts he erected a front structure, on which a tall tower was built in 1713–14 to plans by Jean de Bodt. This tower was to contain the glockenspiel that had been planned for the collapsed "Münzturm" (coin tower), and was therefore built with an open bell storey. But the glockenspiel, the only one in the city, failed to please and was replaced by a new one after only a few years. The local people called the church the "singing clock church" and the glockenspiel was operated by a "glockenist". It was a tourist attraction until it was destroyed in the war.

The church burned down in 1944 and the tower collapsed. Since 1991 the bare interior, which is impressively monumental, has been used as a place of worship and for art events or theatrical performances. A private association is helping to raise money for the reconstruction of the tower.

One of the unluckiest people in the architectural history of Ber-

lin was also involved in the construction of the parochial church:
the court brickmason Leonhard Braun the elder, who was also one
of the wealthiest men of his time. He was largely involved in the
collapse of the rear facade of the Zeughaus and was dismissed;
then he worked on the portal V of the palace and was again dismissed soon afterwards for shoddy workmanship after parts had
broken off from the structure. A few years later, he fitted a solid
dome into the parochial church instead of the planned plank dome,
and as a result the eastern exterior wall collapsed under the
weight. Braun was arrested and compelled to repair the damage
at his own expense. His cousin Leopold then acted as a front man
to continue the construction work.

Baroque
Johann Arnold Nering, Martin Grünberg 1695–1703; tower: Jean de Bodt
1713–14
Mitte, Klosterstrasse 65–67
Open: daily 10–18 hrs., Tel. 247 59 50
www.marienkirche-berlin.de
▷ U Klosterstrasse

Sophienkirche (Queen Sophie Church)

Under the influence of the early evangelical "Pietist" movement, which strove to reconcile Lutheran and Reformed believers and which demanded the greatest simplicity in church design, numerous strikingly plain churches were built during the rule of Friedrich III. / I. Only four of them have survived, and none have retained their original form: the French and German church on Gendarmenmarkt, the ruins of the Parochialkirche and the Sophienkirche.

The Sophienkirche was built as a parish church for the "Spandauer Vorstadt", a suburb that developed irregularly from the end of the 17th century. In 1711 its inhabitants appealed to Queen Sophie Luise, the third wife of Friedrich I., who a year later donated a sum of money sufficient to build a church. According to the will of the king, who had to approve the donation, the suburb was to be given the name "Sophienstadt", but things turned out differently. Sophie Luise fell into a depression in 1712 and her step-son, Friedrich Wilhelm, sent her away to her native region of Mecklenburg after he came to power in 1713. Against the will of the new king, the new church was generally referred to as the "Sophienkirche".

The church was built on a plain rectangular pattern of seven by three axes. The pulpit, altar and font were in a central position in front of the middle of the south wall. Two-storey wooden balconies were erected all around the interior. In 1833 the altar was moved in front of the eastern wall, and the church was fundamentally altered in 1891–92. An apse was added, the ceiling was raised and the entire interior was decorated with neo-baroque ornamentation. The eastern exterior facade was given a curved gable.

The high spire with its elaborate sub-divisions was built in 1732 on the orders and with the finance of King Friedrich Wilhelm. The architect, Johann Friedrich Grael, based it on the collapsed "Münzturm" (coin tower) of the "Stadtschloss" (city palace) designed by Schlüter. Although the king did not really appreciate ceremonious pomp, nevertheless he supported the development of his residence

city, and especially the construction of tall and magnificent church spires – and the Sophienkirche spire is the only one which still survives.

It was only in 1903–05 that an access to the Sophienkirche was created from the west through a splendid ensemble of neo-baroque residential buildings.

Near the Sophienkirche there are still several buildings dating from the 18th and 19th century, some of which have been lovingly restored.

Baroque
Martin Grünberg 1712; spire: Johann Friedrich Grael 1732–34;
alterations: F. Schulze, A. Heyden, K. Bernd 1892
Mitte, Grosse Hamburger Strasse 29
Open: daily 13–18 hrs., Tel. 308 79 20
www.sophien.de
▷ S Hackescher Markt, U Weinmeisterstrasse

Staatsoper (State Opera) Unter den Linden and Hedwigskathedrale (St. Hedwig's Cathedral)

When Friedrich II. came to power in 1740, the city's expansion had been completed. The task now was to fill the available space with splendid structures. The first project was a new city centre, the Forum Fridericianum, which was to combine the arts, science and politics, a concept that was to be symbolised by great architecture.

The first building to be erected was the opera, built in 1741–43, and it was the first free-standing opera house to be built away from the residence of the ruler (photo). The architect was Georg Wenzeslaus von Knobelsdorff, the "surintendant of all royal palaces, houses and gardens". Under Knobelsdorff and Friedrich the Great, rococo interior architecture with its French influence became established in Berlin, but in a more vivacious and sprightly manner, and an elegant and sometimes austere classical baroque was visible in the design of the exterior architecture.

The opera house was originally a simple rectangular building to which a magnificent portal was added, as well as narrow projections with outdoor steps and columns. Several phases of alteration drastically changed the exterior, for example after a fire in 1843 and fundamental alterations in 1926. The heavily protruding central projections on the long sides and the box-shaped stage tower were added, but in the restoration from 1952–55 based on plans by Richard Paulick the stage tower was given a facade structure that appeared almost original. The elongated rectangular floor plan was based on the idea of a temple of Apollo. The figures on the exterior depict poets of antiquity and figures from Greek mythology. The interior design dates from the 1950s, and is based on Knobelsdorff's original design. By 2013 the building will be renovated; the auditorium's ceiling will be raised and the space's acoustics improved.

The second building, which was not part of the original plan, was the Hedwig Cathedral, which was built behind the opera house as the church for Catholics, the population of which had increased by this time. With this building, the king also wanted to demonstrate

his religious tolerance – after he had acquired the Catholic region of Silesia. Here, again, he chose a famous model, in this case the Pantheon of ancient Rome, and he drew the first sketches which Knobelsdorff then worked out in detail. The building work was carried out from 1747–55 by Johann Boumann and was more or less provisionally completed in 1771–73. After damage in the war, the present cathedral of the Catholic archbishop was rebuilt with a slightly altered dome and a completely redesigned interior (designed by Hans Schippert). The floor opens up to a wide staircase down to the crypt, and the upper and lower church are linked by an altar column.

Baroque
State opera: Georg Wenzeslaus von Knobelsdorff 1741–43; altered several times; Reconstruction: Richard Paulick 1952–55;
Hedwigskathedrale: Georg Wenzeslaus von Knobelsdorff, Johann Boumann 1747–55
Mitte, Unter den Linden 5–7 / Bebelplatz
Open (cathedral): daily 8–17 hrs., Sun & holidays 13–17 hrs.,
Tel. 203 48 10
www.hedwigs-kathedrale.de / www.staatsoper-berlin.de
▷ U Französische Strasse, bus 100

Humboldt-Universität (Humboldt University) and Alte Bibliothek (Old Library)

The third building in the Forum Fridericianum was the palace of Prince Heinrich, the brother of Friedrich II., which was built in 1748–66. The original concept was for a new royal palace, but by this time Friedrich had lost interest in Berlin and stayed as often as possible in Potsdam, especially in his newly built pleasure palace Sanssouci. The design was possibly by Knobelsdorff, who had now fallen into disfavour, and the building work was directed by Johann Boumann and Carl Ludwig Hildebrandt.

Seven years after the prince died, the building was assigned to the newly founded Friedrich Wilhelm University which started its lecturing activities in 1810 (the name was changed to "Humboldt University" after the Second World War). The formerly rich adornment was reduced over time, apart from the festive hall which was destroyed in the war.

The original palace was a three-wing complex grouped around the courtyard of honour facing the Linden boulevard. The end structures facing Lindenallee had seven window axes. In 1913–20, Ludwig Hoffmann widened the originally narrow wings to the width of these end buildings and extended them far to the north, thus creating an elongated second courtyard.

The complex is accentuated by the central projection and the projections of the end buildings which contain statues. The Corinthian column structure of the central projection is similar to the opera house. The flat roof is almost concealed by the surrounding balustrade. The solid impression is heightened by the block-like structure of the three storeys, and the middle storey is emphasised by the high round arch windows. The angled gateway pillars with groups of children are worth noting.

The western side of the Forum is occupied by the "Kommode" (chest of drawers), so called because of its rounded forms, which was used for the royal library which was founded in 1661 by the Great Elector and had until then been accommodated in the

palace. At the command of the king, Georg Christian Unger copied the 50 years older design of Fischer von Erlach for the Hofburg in Vienna, although the Hofburg was only completed in 1889–93 and in an altered form. Thus, curiously, the copy is older than its model, and closer to the original design. In contrast to the four-storey facade structure, the interior only has two storeys. Following its destruction in the war, the library was rebuilt by 1969; the exterior is a replica of the original, the inside a modern design. Since 1914 the building has been used by the university and now houses the faculty of law.

Baroque
Humboldt University, former Prince Heinrich palace: Johann Boumann, Carl Ludwig Hildebrandt 1748–66; extended by Ludwig Hoffmann 1913–20
Old library / chest of drawers: Georg Christian Unger after a design by Fischer von Erlach 1775–80
Mitte, Unter den Linden 6 / Bebelplatz
www.hu-berlin.de
▷ U Französische Strasse, S / U Friedrichstrasse, bus 100

Ephraim-Palais (Ephraim Palace)

The home of the rich banker and coin merchant Veitel Heine Ephraim, built in 1762–65 by Friedrich Wilhelm Diterichs on the corner of Molkenmarkt, was regarded as the "most beautiful corner in Berlin". The Molkenmarkt, which is today cut off from its urban context by the wide Mühlendamm road, was formerly one of the central squares in Berlin. Ephraim was a Jew, and as the financier of Friedrich the Great during the Seven Years' War he obtained the rights of Christian merchants here. It was only because of this that he was able to purchase land which had been a domain of the patricians since the Middle ages, and build on it. In 1762 he purchased the building at Poststrasse 16 and had it completely redesigned by Friedrich Wilhelm Diterichs, who previously designed the palace church in Buch and the princess palace. The task was difficult because of the oblique angle at which the two wings of the building met. Diterichs solved the problem in the interior by creating two oval rooms one behind the other. On the outside he underlined the corner by the double columns. The first floor balcony, which links the three window axes on the corner, can be reached through large French doors and has gold-plated balcony rails and sculptures. The second storey has individual balconies, and the upper storey only has one balcony for the middle window.

In 1935 the palace had to make way for road widening work, but after protests from the population the facade was removed brick by brick and stored in the district of Wedding, and brought back to Molkenmarkt in 1983. The palace was completely reconstructed up to 1987, although it was now 12 metres further back. The interior rooms were decorated with a simplified rococo ornamentation, and they are now used as exhibition rooms for the city museum.

Another building worth viewing is the Ermelerhaus, which was originally in Breite Strasse and was also altered by Diterichs in 1760 and fitted with splendid rococo interior ornamentation. The

facade was altered in the classical style in 1804. It was the only house in the row to survive the war, and in 1968–69 it was moved to the historic row of houses on the bank of the Spree.

Also worth taking a look at is the Magnushaus opposite the Pergamon Museum that originates from the 1750s and is believed to go back to a design by Knobelsdorff. In 1842 Gustav Magnus established the first physics laboratory in Germany here. In 1912–28 the theatre director Max Reinhardt lived on the top floor. The left wing of the building, facing Dorotheenstrasse, was added later and exhibits classical ornamentation.

Baroque
Friedrich Wilhelm Diterichs 1762–66; rebuilt by Franz Klinger 1983–87
Mitte, Poststrasse 16, on the corner of Mühlendamm
Open: Tues–Sun 10–18 hrs., Wed 12–20 hrs., Tel. 24 00 21 62
www.stadtmuseum.de
▷ U Klosterstrasse, S / U Alexanderplatz

Deutscher Dom (German Dome Church) and Französischer Dom (French Dome Church)

In the creation of the grid-like street layout of Friedrichstadt after 1688, the central area was the Friedrichstadt market, and two churches were built next to it. To the north was the French church for the Huguenot community in Berlin, which had grown considerably after the Edict of Potsdam of 1685 (the first of five French parish churches built in Berlin up to 1800), which Louis Cayart modelled on the main church of the Huguenots in Charenton near Paris which had been destroyed in 1688. To the south of the market, the "Neue Kirche" (new church) was built (which was only later referred to as the German church), for which Martin Grünberg developed a unique five-sided central structure based on the floor plan of the Parochialkirche. A tower structure was planned to the west, but it did not get beyond the basement.

In 1774, Friedrich the Great decided to enlarge the square and make it more attractive. On the western side he had a small French comedy theatre built. He commissioned Carl von Gontard to build two non-functional domes for the existing churches to create a festive context for the comedy theatre. The models were the Piazza del Popolo in Rome and the ensembles by Christopher Wren and Inigo Jones in London. Three-storey residential buildings were built in the surrounding area.

The identical domes were built in 1780–85 and had no inner connection with the churches. The French dome church was partly used by the French community and has been the home of the Huguenot museum since 1929; the Berlin Historical Association was later accommodated in the German dome church (photo).

In 1881 / 82 the German church, which was in a poor state of repair, was completely rebuilt on the old floor plan, and in the process the truncated tower to the west was removed and the exterior was adapted to the dome architecture. The church and tower burned out in 1943, were completely rebuilt in the interior and only reopened in 1996 for the permanent exhibition "Milestones, Setbacks and

Sidetracks. The Path of Parliamentary Democracy in Germany".
The interior of the French church was completely redesigned by
Otto March in 1905, and he created a three-axis central projection
on the plain west facade. The church was also destroyed in 1943
and restored in 1978–83 in keeping with the ideas of March. Instead
of the balconies, however, an intermediate floor was added so
that now, as the former exterior hinted, there are two rooms one
above the other.

Baroque
French church: Louis Cayart 1701–05; alterations: Otto March 1905;
partition into two rooms 1978–83
German church: Martin Grünberg 1701–08; alterations 1881 / 82
H.v.d. Hude, J. Hennicke; new interior design
Towers: Carl von Gontard, Georg Christian Unger 1780–85
Mitte, Gendarmenmarkt
Open: French church: Tues–Sun 12–17 hrs., Tel. 20 64 99 22;
German church (Milestones, Setbacks and Sidetracks): Tues–Sun
10–18 hrs., Tel. 22 73 04 31
www.französischer-dom.de / www.bundestag.de
▷ U Stadtmitte, U Französische Strasse

Die Stadtpalais (The Town Palaces)
Unter den Linden

Along Unter den Linden there are a number of palaces built by the nobility that are worth a closer look. They are all on the southern side of the street and can be seen from the Neue Wache.

The building at Unter den Linden 1 is the newest and most controversial. It was built in 2000–04 by Thomas van den Valentyn. The facade design of the front and the two narrow sides is based completely on the residential and administrative building of Berlin's garrison (interior from 1653 by Memhardt, facades from 1795/96 by Wilhelm Konrad Titel), which is why the building is called the "old commander" or "commander's house." The back facade and the interior, however, are modern designs.

The Kronprinzenpalais (Crown Prince Palace, photo) was reconstructed in 1968/69 after it had burned down in the war and been cleared away later. Originally built in 1663–69 as the private house of a court secretary, it was converted by Philipp Gerlach in 1733 as a town palace for Crown Prince Friedrich. It was then greatly altered by Heinrich Strack in 1856–57 for the later Emperor Friedrich III. Strack added with classical ornaments. From 1919 to 1937, the building housed the modern department of the National Gallery.

The neighbouring Prinzessinnenpalais (Princess Palace), also a reconstruction, is now the opera café. Its main facade faces Oberwallstrasse, where Friedrich Wilhelm Diterichs connected two existing buildings in 1833 to create a large palace. In 1810 the end building by Heinrich Gentz created a fine facade facing Linden Boulevard. For the new residents, the daughters of the king, a covered bridge was built to the palace of their brother, the Crown Prince.

On the corner of Lindenforum and Unter den Linden, the town palace of Crown Prince Wilhelm was built from 1834–37, and Wilhelm lived there as the king and the first German Emperor until his death. The architect was Karl Ferdinand Langhans, the son of the architect

of the Brandenburg Gate. Instead of an intricate design by Schinkel, a classically austere sandstone building was built. The small windows of a low third floor (mezzanine) are concealed by a terracotta frieze. The middle of the building is emphasised by a balcony supported by pillars. The rear wing of the palace extended far into the block of buildings beyond the Alte Bibliothek (Old Library).

Next to it is the facade of the former governor's building of 1721 which was removed from its original location near the town hall on the corner of Jüdenstrasse in 1960 and reconstructed here.

Baroque / Classicism
Alte Kommandantur: Th. van den Valentyn 2000–04, after the design by Wilhelm Konrad Titel 1795 / 96
Kronprinzenpalais: Ph. Gerlach 1732; J.H. Strack 1856 / 57; R. Paulick 1968 / 69;
Kronprinzessinnenpalais: F.W. Diterichs 1733; H. Gentz 1810 / 11;
R. Paulick 1963 / 64
Altes Palais: Karl Ferdinand Langhans 1834–37
Governor's house: F.W. Diterichs and M. Böhme 1721; 1963 / 64 Meinhardt
Mitte, Unter den Linden
▷ U Französische Strasse, bus 100

Schloss Bellevue (Bellevue Palace)

A year before the death of Friedrich the Great, Classisicm finally became established in Prussia. Bellevue palace was the first classical palace building in Prussia; its three-wing basic structure is baroque in style, but its austere facade is clearly classical. In just one year, 1785, the palace was erected under the direction of Philipp Daniel Boumann as a summer residence for the youngest brother of the king, August Ferdinand. Until 1918 it was lived in by the Hohenzollern family, and from 1935–38 it served as a museum of ethnology. Then, after extensive alterations by Paul Baumgarten, who completely redesigned the interior, it was used as the guest house of the government. After heavy war damage it was rebuilt in its old form, but again with a changed interior. Only the oval room, which was built in 1791 by Carl Gotthard Langhans, was preserved. Since 1959 the palace has been used as the Berlin headquarters of the Federal Presidents, and since 1993 as their main official residence.

The three-wing complex is clearly dominated by the central wing because of its size and ornamentation. The two-storey main building extends through 19 window axes, and the centre is marked by a three-axis projecting section. A triangular gable is supported on Corinthian projecting columns and contains allegorical representations of agriculture, fish farming and hunting, in keeping with a summer residence outside the city gates. The entrance, which is emphasised by outdoor steps, was only added in 1938. Previously the building had two portals in the central axes of the two only slightly protruding corner projections, as can still be seen today by the shape of the openings and the roofs.

The two plain side wings, which are low in spite of their three storeys, appear to be simply added on (and are referred to as the ladies' wing and the Spree wing). The front three of the total of 16 axes have just two storeys, which creates the overall impression that the structures rise towards the central structure.

The facade facing the garden differs especially in the stronger emphasis of the corner projections and the continuous roof eaves without any gables.

To the south of the palace, in the park which is not accessible to the public, the four-storey office building of the Federal President has been built in the form of an ellipse (1996–98, Martin Gruber, Helmut Kleine-Kranenburg). The windows are set into the dark green polished granite facade without any ornamentation.

Classicism
Philipp Daniel Boumann 1785
Tiergarten, Spreeweg 1
▷ S Bellevue, bus 100

Brandenburger Tor (Brandenburg Gate)

The position of the Brandenburg Gate was "of its kind undisputedly the most beautiful in the whole world" and therefore he took the Propylaeum on the Acropolis in Athens "as the model", as Carl Gotthard Langhans wrote on his design which was implemented in 1789–91. The present emblem of the city was only one of a total of 18 city gates; the position and names of the other gates can often still be seen on a street map. But this gate was by far the most elaborate – most gates just consisted of two simple pillars. Construction work began in the year of the French Revolution, and it was the first building in Berlin's architectural history to be based on models from Greek antiquity – a trend which eventually led Berlin to be called "Athens on the Spree". The gate with its angled side wings (the guard houses) originally joined directly onto the city wall, but when the city wall was demolished in 1867–68, pedestrian passages were created in the side halls and column halls were built in front of the plain western front.

The gate has five openings which are eleven metres in depth and separated by walls, and their ends are covered by Doric columns. Above the Doric entablature and the steps of the attic is the five metre high copper "Quadriga" with the goddess of victory, designed by Gottfried Schadow and cast in bronze by Emanuel Jury. The goddess Victoria is shown in reliefs as a bringer of peace, and a time of peace is portrayed as a time of cultural abundance. Originally, it was even suggested that the gate should be entitled "Peace Gate". The central figure in the reliefs of the openings through the gate is Heracles.

In its design, the gate reverses the significance of mediaeval city gates, in that it represents the openness and cultural generosity of the self-assured city of residence.

In 1807 the Quadriga was taken away to Paris by Napoleon, but in 1814 it was brought back in a triumphal procession. After the structure had thus become a symbol of victory in the liberation

wars, Schinkel added an iron cross to the crown on the rod of the goddess of victory. After war damage, the gate was restored in the 1950s, and with the renovated Quadriga (which was again restored in 1990 / 91), the gate spent the years from 1961 to 1989 in no-man's-land close to the Wall to West Berlin.

The gate was originally integrated into the continuous complex of buildings around the rectangular Pariser Platz, but in and after the Second World War all of the other buildings disappeared apart from remains of the Academy of Arts. Begun in 1995, reconstruction of Pariser Platz in its historical dimensions is now complete. The residential buildings which once joined the gate at the sides, i.e. the house of the painter Max Liebermann to the north and Haus Sommer to the south, have been rebuilt in simplified historical form (by Josef Paul Kleihues based on the original design of August Stüler).

Classicism
Carl Gotthard Langhans 1789–91, "Quadriga" by Gottfried Schadow
Mitte, Pariser Platz
▷ S / U Brandenburger Tor, bus 100

Pfaueninsel (Peacock Island)

The whole of Peacock Island was conceived as a work of art. In 1793 King Friedrich Wilhelm II. bought it as an excursion venue and made it into an exotic world. He and his successor Friedrich Wilhelm III. had the island designed as a park, built a palace at the south-west end and had small buildings and scenic highlights created at many points on the island. All of the apparently natural clearings, groups of trees and lines of sight were artistically planted or cleared. Characteristic features are the winding pathways which create constantly new views of natural beauties or architectural delicacies. Furthermore, exotic species were planted, a rose garden and a flower garden were created and a considerable animal collection was established which formed the basis of the Berlin zoo in 1842.

Although it had long been a popular place for trips, Peacock Island was only rarely used by the royal family after the death of Friedrich Wilhelm III. in 1840.

The palace is a wooden building by the court joiner Johann Gottlieb Brendel which is designed as a "ruined Roman country mansion". Two round towers frame a ruin-like middle section and are connected by a bridge. The oak beams are covered by a painted hewn stone pattern, and an illusionist landscape painting adorns the door. The bridge was originally made of wood, but in 1807 it was replaced by the present cast iron bridge, the first of its kind in Berlin. The facade, which is designed almost as a stage prop, was designed for the effect it creates at a distance when seen from the Marble Palace in Potsdam, the main residence of Friedrich Wilhelm II.

Inside the palace is the only undamaged interior from the king's period in power, probably furnished by his main mistress, Countess Lichtenau, who had travelled to Italy in 1795 / 96 and brought back numerous souvenirs.

At the northern tip of the island, Brendel built the diary as an

artificial ruin in Gothic forms. He built a nearby stable in the form of a chapel. The Kavaliershaus (cavalier's house – a guest house) in its present form is a radical alteration by Schinkel (1824–26). The facade of a late Gothic patrician house in Danzig was built into the tower, the rest of the facade was in the Gothic style. The Swiss house at the southern tip of the island, which was also built to Schinkel's plans in 1829–30, was a classical variation of the Swiss house motif which was in vogue at the time (several examples survive in nearby Klein-Glienicke). The island also has a number of other picturesque buildings.

Neo-Gothic (Classical period)
Various buildings: Johann Gottlieb Brendel, Karl Friedrich Schinkel and others, 1794–1830
Zehlendorf, Pfaueninsel, Nikolskoer Weg
Open: island: May–Sept Tues–Sun 10–18 hrs., Oct Tues–Sun 10–17 hrs.;
palace: May–Aug daily 8–21 hrs., Sept–Oct daily 9–18 hrs.;
Tel. 80 58 68 31
www.spsg.de
▷ Bus 218

Neue Wache (New Guardhouse)

When it was built in 1818, the Neue Wache was the first independent work by a 37 year old architect who was to become the dominant figure in the architecture of Berlin and Prussia in the following decades, and is still honoured today: Karl Friedrich Schinkel. He was a successful painter, stage designer, theorist, monument conservationist and city planner, and he became a close and influential companion of the artistically minded crown prince, Friedrich Wilhelm IV. He created an impressive range of architectural works – although some are now lost – and his ideas and designs can be seen throughout the region. Schinkel's classicism remained the dominant architectural style in Berlin until about 1870.

The Neue Wache was the first representational building of the state to be erected after the French occupation, and although it was used as a simple guardhouse, it was regarded as a monument to the "wars of liberation". Schinkel succeeded in giving this small building between the large complexes of the Zeughaus and the university its own identity. The castle-type corner projections give the simple rectangular structure a solidity and stability which are underlined by the accentuated pedestal. The two-row Doric hall of columns beneath the gable opens the building towards Unter den Linden and gives it depth. The gable shows allegories of war, and the frieze is decorated with a sculpted portrayal of victories by Schadow. The original plans by Schinkel included statues of the generals Bülow and Scharnhorst (by Christian Daniel Rauch) at each side, which can now be seen opposite the building.

In 1918 the Neue Wache lost its function, and in 1930 / 31 it was converted by Heinrich Tessenow for use as a simple memorial to those killed in the war. From 1960 onwards it was used as a memorial for the victims of fascism and militarism, and since 1993 the building, in a reconstruction of Tessenow's design and with an enlarged copy of the sculpture "Mourning mother with dead

son" by Käthe Kollwitz, has become the central memorial site of the Federal Republic of Germany.

Behind the so-called "wood of chestnut trees" is the former "Palais Donner" built in 1751–53 by Christian Friedrich Feldmann, now known as the "Palais am Festungsgraben" (palace by the fortress moat). In 1808 it was used by the Ministry of Finance; in 1861–63 the three storey building was completely rebuilt and given a late classical facade. In 1934 the festival hall from the demolished Weydingerhaus, which was probably fitted and decorated by Schinkel, was moved into the Palais Donner.

Next to it and set further back is the former singing academy, now the Maxim Gorki theatre, a building by Carl Theodor Ottmer to a design by Schinkel which was built in 1824–27, restored with a new interior in 1946–47.

Classicism
Karl Friedrich Schinkel 1816–18
Mitte, Unter den Linden
▷ U Französische Strasse, bus 100

Schauspielhaus /Konzerthaus
(Playhouse /Concert Hall)

In 1774–76, Friedrich the Great had a small French comedy theatre built on Gendarmenmarkt, and towards the end of the 18th century under August Wilhelm Iffland it became the "Nationaltheater" and the leading German theatre. As early as 1800 / 01, Carl Gotthard Langhans built a new, larger theatre which now had to match the architecture of the dome towers of the German and French churches (cf. p. 50f.). But in 1817 the building burned down to its outside walls, and a year later Schinkel was commissioned to design a new building.

Schinkel was bound by a number of requirements stipulated by the king. For example, the old exterior walls and the portico columns were to be retained, and the auditorium was to be reduced to create space for an additional concert hall and other ancillary rooms. Schinkel solved the task brilliantly. He retained the basic ground layout of the Langhans building which was at right angles to the square, but converted it to a three-part structure with a higher and wider central structure. With the aid of an outdoor flight of steps, the Ionic portico and a top gable crowned with statues on the central structure, he created a majestic, steep facade which became the central element dominating Gendarmenmarkt. The side ends have very wide gables, and the rear facade mirrors the front but with slight recesses.

Whereas the ashlar masonry blocks of the pedestal follow traditional forms, the geometrical pattern of the wall surfaces in the two main storeys was completely new. The projections at the corners spanning both storeys, the gable facades at the sides and the single storey projections on the wall facades create a framework into which the windows and wall panels are recessed. The rich sculpted ornamentation was created by Friedrich Tieck and Christian Rauch. The walls originally had a rendered finish, but in 1881 the building was clad with sandstone facing blocks. The northern part of the building contained the functional rooms, the

south contained the concert hall. The central structure contained the theatre with seats for 1200. The semi-circular auditorium had rising stalls and two balconies with boxes behind them. The auditorium was redesigned in the baroque style in 1903 / 04.

After war damage, the exterior was reconstructed true to the original, but the interior was completely redesigned. Instead of a theatre with a stage, a concert auditorium with 1850 seats was built, based in its form and decor on Schinkel's small concert hall, which was once located in the south wing. The ceremonial opening was in 1984. Since 1994 the building has been known as "Konzerthaus Berlin".

Classicism
Karl Friedrich Schinkel 1918–21, interior architecture: K. Just, M. Prasser 1979–84
Mitte, Gendarmenmarkt
www.konzerthaus.de
▷ U Stadtmitte, U Französische Strasse

Friedrichswerdersche Kirche
(Friedrichswerder Church)

Karl Friedrich Schinkel created many church designs for Berlin, but he only actually built five: four classical buildings in the northern suburbs – Nazarethkirche in Wedding, St. Paul in Gesundbrunnen, St. Johannis in Moabit, and St. Elisabeth in Mitte – and Friedrichswerder parish church, the first neo-Gothic church building in Berlin which thus set a new trend. The previous church had become derelict, and Schinkel designed a new building in the form of a Roman temple. However, at the suggestion of the king he then decided to build in the "mediaeval style". His reasoning seems strange to modern visitors: he said that this style fitted "into this rather narrow district of the city which is similar to antiquity with the irregularity of its streets". The twin tower front of the church originally towered high above the small, densely built market of this first baroque extension of the city.

The design was based on Gothic church buildings, but in the clear, cubic structure of the building and the facade it shows a clearly classical sense of form. For the construction of the building, which was supervised by Ludwig Ferdinand Hesse, Schinkel chose bare brick, the typical feature of Gothic buildings in the Mark Brandenburg – and thus started a Gothic renaissance.

The church is a single-aisle building with five piers and a five-sided chancel polygon, and with buttresses which reach low into the interior, are interrupted in the lower part and have balconies with pointed arch arcades inserted between them. The piers are cross-vaulted, but painted sandstone lierne ribs create the illusion of stellar vaults.

The exterior is based on English chapel architecture. Characteristic features include not only the blunt towers but also the high wide windows and the shallow slope of the roof which is concealed by tracery. The flat exterior buttresses end in small pinnacles.

All interior and exterior ornamentation is of baked terracotta. The two cast-iron leaf-type doors were based on models by Fried-

rich Tieck and Ludwig Wilhelm Wichmann. After the war, the church was a ruin for many years. Since its restoration in 1982–87 it has been used as an exhibition room for a collection of classical sculptures.

Another important building by Schinkel, the "Bauakademie" (Building Academy), which was next to the church on the Spree side, was demolished after the war to make room for the Foreign Ministry of the GDR. There have been plans to reconstruct the Building Academy since its demolition in 1995. Although the project once seemed close to realization, it's fate is now totally uncertain due to a lack of funding.

Neo-Gothic (classical period)
Karl Friedrich Schinkel, Ludwig Ferdinand Hesse (building supervision)
1824–31
Mitte, Werderscher Markt
Open: daily 10–18 hrs., Tel. 208 13 23
▷ U Hausvogteiplatz, bus 100, 147

Altes Museum (Old Museum)

At the northern tip of the island on the Spree in Cölln, which was too marshy to build on in the Middle Ages, the Great Elector had a palace park with a botanical garden created, and this park was named "Lustgarten" (pleasure garden). When the fortifications were built in the 17th century the area was divided and the soldier king made the "Lustgarten" into a military parade ground. When the desire for a public museum arose in 1815 as a result of the exhibition of art treasures recovered from the French forces that had previously plundered them, Schinkel suggested the site to the north of the "Lustgarten" as a worthy site. A ditch which formed part of the old fortifications was therefore filled in, and the first dedicated museum building in Berlin was built on wooden piles from 1825–30.

The rectangular building complex encloses two inner courtyards and a central rotunda spanning two storeys, with block-type outer walls which rise above the rest of the building. The south of the building facing the Lustgarten, which is unsuitable as a source of lighting for the paintings, opens up its entire width into a portico of Ionic columns. Behind the wide outdoor flight of steps, five axes of the portico open into the depth of the building where two stair-cases on both sides of the entrance lead to the upper storey. The imaginative concept of merging the outdoor and indoor areas was unfortunately spoiled in the 1990s by the addition of a glass front which separates the staircase hall.

Two groups of statutes, an Amazon and a lion fighter by August Kiss and Albert Wolff, decorate the outdoor steps. The rotunda in the interior, which is based on the rotundas in the Vatican muse-ums, contains sculptures of gods of antiquity in its wall recesses.

A few days before the end of the war, when the museum was already damaged, a tank truck exploded nearby and the museum was burned out completely. The building was reconstructed in 1966, but on the inside only the rotunda was recreated in its original form.

The large granite bowl in front of the museum was once intended to be mounted in the rotunda, but the stonemason G.C. Cantian went to the limit of what was technically possible and extended its diameter to seven metres, which was too big for the rotunda. The boulder originates from a field stone found near Fürstenwalde, where it was upturned by 100 men, hauled through the forest and transported to Berlin by boat on the Spree. At the ceremonial breakfast to dedicate this "wonder of the world" in 1834, 42 people sat around the edge of the bowl.

In 1935 the bowl was moved to a position to the north of the "Dom" (cathedral), and when it was being moved back in 1981 it broke apart. It was joined together again, but the crack can still be clearly seen.

Classicism
Karl Friedrich Schinkel 1825–30
Mitte, Am Lustgarten
Open: daily 10–18 hrs., Thurs 10–22 hrs., Tel. 20 90 50
www.smb.museum
▷ S Hackescher Markt, bus 100

Schloss Klein-Glienicke
(Klein-Glienicke Palace)

The Klein-Glienicke palace complex is impressive in its coherence and its compact variety. Although it is within the Berlin city boundaries, it clearly belongs to the Potsdam residence scenery, and there are many lines of sight to the neighbouring Babelsberg Palace, to the Nikolaikirche in Potsdam and to the Heilandkirche in Sacrow.

Klein-Glienicke palace was developed from the estate house of Glienicke hunting palace which was built to the south of Königstrasse for Crown Prince Friedrich in 1682. The hunting palace, which was altered in the baroque style in the 19th century, was completely hollowed out and altered – to its detriment – by Max Taut in 1963. It is now used as a conference centre. In 1824 the estate that was laid out to the north was acquired by Prince Karl, the brother of Friedrich Wilhelm IV, and Karl had the estate house made into a splendid summer residence.

The former estate of Klein-Glienicke had already been built as a splendid structure by its previous owner, and it acquired its present appearance under Schinkel from 1825–28. It is an irregular three-wing complex which is unobtrusively adapted to the surrounding scenery with restrained, strictly classical forms. Above the central projection of the main facade was a balcony which enabled the occupants to take tea and enjoy the view. The eastern wing was raised by one storey by Ludwig Persius in 1844. The single-storey cavalier house with its characteristic overhanging roof (with a stable below and a visitors' dwelling above) bounds the inner courtyard, and together with the carriage house it forms an additional courtyard. The tower was originally designed by Schinkel but an extra storey was added later.

There followed the Orangerie by Persius and the monastic court (by Ferdinand von Arnim, around 1850), which accommodated the mediaeval collection of the art-loving prince in its Byzantine cloister architecture.

Above the banks of the Havel rises the casino by Schinkel, an austere two-storey rendered building with projecting pergolas; the upper storey was once used as a guest house. Further to the north along the bank, the steam machine house is linked with the gardener's house which is impressively set into the sloping bank and opens the way to the extensive rear section of the park, the present "Volkspark" (public park).

Many details in the grounds, including numerous wooden buildings, have been lost (especially due to alterations in the 1950s). But there are still many buildings and sculptures to be discovered, including the "Gasthaus Moorlake" which was built by Persius in 1841 as a forester's lodge in the popular Swiss style.

Classicism
Karl Friedrich Schinkel, Ludwig Persius, Ferdinand von Arnim 1825 to about 1850
Zehlendorf, Königstrasse 36
Open: April–Oct Tues–Sun 10–18 hrs., Nov–March Sat, Sun & holidays 10–17 hrs., Tel. 80 58 67 50
www.spsg.de
▷ Bus 316

Blockhaus Nikolskoe and St. Peter and Paul

In honour of a visit by his daughter Charlotte and her husband, the later Russian czar Nikolaus, King Friedrich Wilhelm III. had the "Blockhaus" built in 1819 in the style of Russian farmhouses. He gave it as a gift to his son-in-law, and the name means "belonging to Nikolaus". Due to its picturesque setting high above the Havel it is a popular excursion venue today. After a fire in 1984 it was rebuilt true to the original.

The two storey building with its overhanging ridge roof is made of massive beams which interlock at the corners. The window and door frames are ornamentally decorated with forms that are in some cases still baroque in style.

Not far from Nikolskoe, the church of St. Peter and Paul (photo) was built in 1834–87. The king expected "designs in the style of Russian churches but with only one tower", but August Stüler and his assistant Albert Dietrich Schadow, the son of the famous sculptor, ignored this instruction and designed a building which was similar to the suburban churches designed by Schinkel in 1832. The Russian onion-shaped dome, the terrace and the high western facade were added at the suggestion of Schinkel and the crown prince.

The exterior of the cubic building is plain. The smooth wall surfaces are divided into two horizontal bands by a horizontal ledge and contain four round arched windows set in a row of window recesses. The solid western wall rises above the eaves height of the nave, but in the upper section it contains arcades which make it less massive in appearance. The slender tower has two octagonal storeys topped by an onion-shaped dome.

The interior is particularly interesting for art historians because it is the only church interior in Berlin that is preserved from the classical period. It, too, is plain in appearance with its clear forms, the flat beam ceiling and the galleries, but its colours make it bright and attractive.

The two mosaic medallions on the pulpit with images of the saints who gave the church its name are Roman works from the 18th century which Pope Clemens XIII. gave as a gift to Friedrich the Great.

Russian block house style / classicism
Blockhaus Nikolskoe: pioneer guards battalion under Captain Snethlage 1819; St. Peter and Paul: August Stüler and Albert Dietrich Schadow 1834–37
Zehlendorf, Nikolskoer Weg 17
Open: church: daily 11–16 hrs., Tel. 805 21 00; blockhouse: 805 29 14
▷ Bus 218

Tierärztliche Hochschule
(College of Veterinary Medicine)

In the shadow of the tower block of the Charité hospital is the spreading complex of the veterinary department of the Humboldt University. Here, where the Panke stream comes to the surface for the last time before it runs into the Spree below ground level, there is a hidden architectural jewel: the "Trichinentempel", officially the former anatomical theatre of the veterinary college, which was built in 1789 / 90 by Carl Gotthard Langhans. The two-storey rendered building has a square ground layout with projecting central sections spanning three window axes and a gable over the portal. At the centre of the building, surrounded by laboratory rooms, is the lecture room (now No. 8) which is marked in the exterior by the broad tambour with the shallow dome. The square lower windows are linked with the first floor high round arch windows by a balustrade. The former purpose of the building is indicated by the ox skulls on the arch bricks of the top windows. At the top of the facade, a Doric triglyph frieze runs around the building, corresponding in style with the two columns of the portal.

The interior of the lecture room – which is unfortunately usually locked – is unusual. The steep rising rows of seats and Gothic style balustrades are part of the original design, and the same also applies to the paintings on the dome which show motifs such as shepherds and country people with pets. In 1874 a second building was added with the same forms.

The main building of the veterinary college, which is also now used by the veterinary department of the Humboldt University, is more recent in origin. It was built in 1839 / 40 to plans by Ludwig Hesse in the classical forms of the Schinkel school. The three-wing complex encloses a court of honour on the Luisenstrasse side. The straight window structure and the ledges between the three storeys emphasise the horizontal, so that the projecting gabled central section with its round arch windows spanning two storeys appears all the more massive and ceremonious.

On the other side of Luisenstrasse is the extensive complex of the Charité, the famous hospital which goes back to an institute founded by Friedrich the Great. It consists of a large number of free-standing neo-Gothic brick buildings dating from the turn of the century. The surgery tower with operating theatres and hospital wards was built in 1977–82.

The former suburb of Friedrich-Wilhelm-Stadt also contains the Deutsches Theater and a number of early 19th century residential buildings, e.g. in a row of terraced houses in Marienstrasse.

Classicism
Main building: Ludwig Hesse 1839 / 40; Anatomy: Carl Gotthard Langhans 1789 / 90
Mitte, Luisenstrasse 56
▷ S / U Friedrichstrasse, bus 147

Neues Museum (New Museum)

After he came to power in 1840, Friedrich Wilhelm IV. began to implement his plans to create "a site for art and science" on the northern end of the Spree island and to exhibit the scattered royal collections. The first building to be constructed after the Old Museum – renamed this in 1841 – was the New Museum, designed by Friedrich August Stüler. By 1852 the first sections were finished, but the building was only completed in 1866.

Stüler is considered the most important Berlin architect of post-Schinkel classicism, and the New Museum is, without a doubt, his masterpiece. His goal was to create a didactic world of experience, which was intended to educate and "elevate" visitors, as well as impress and intrigue them.

The New Museum was built as a complement to the Old Museum. It was intended to provide space for many, often heavy pieces without interfering with the planned temple. This is why the New Museum appears monumental without being superior. With its clear, plastered facades, it appears noble and reserved. In its floor plan Stüler copied that of Schinkel's building: The New Museum is a rectangular structure with a middle section and two courtyards. The three exhibition floors are accessed via a central stairway, which also dominates the building's exterior – as a high, expansive, windowed middle section, which protrudes on the longer sides, dominating these with its flat, sculpture-ornamented pediment. The east side is contained by two corner structures with flat domes: From the south cupola hall on the first floor a bridge once crossed over to the Old Museum. The stones of the brick building were plastered and hewed.

From a structural point of view this was an extremely modern complex. The entire building has a substructure made of cast and wrought iron girders, some of which were state of the art at the time. The glass roof over the Egyptian Courtyard was the first of its kind in Berlin – an element that later led the great department stores to flourish.

The building was severely damaged in 1945, and efforts to restore what had become a ruin were only begun in 1999. Following lengthy discussions it was decided that the new structure would be neither a reconstruction of the old nor a new building. Instead, the plans of the British architect, David Chipperfield, ensured that existing parts of the building would be secured and kept and the missing parts would be modern in their design. This led to situations like that found, for instance, in the central staircase, where the original bare brick walls abut on the exposed concrete of the new stairs. The reconstructed building was opened in October 2009.

Classicism
August Stüler 1841–66
Mitte, Bodestrasse (museum island)
Open: Sun–Weds 10–18 hrs., Thurs–Sat 10–22 hrs., Tel. 266 42 42 42
www.neues-museum.de
▷ S Hackescher Markt, bus 100

St. Matthäuskirche (St. Matthew Church)

With the enormous growth in the population of Berlin in the 19th century there was also a growing need for new parish churches. The most productive church architect in the middle decades of the century, and one of the major architects in the period after Schinkel, was Schinkel's former pupil August Stüler, who also succeeded him as the head of the Prussian high building deputation. One of his most beautiful church buildings – and at least topographically outstanding – is the Matthäuskirche in what is now the "Kulturforum".

From the end of the 1830s, the affluent citizens of Berlin were attracted westwards to the southern edge of the Tiergarten park where the so-called "privy councillor district" gradually developed on the basis of a detailed development plan. At the suggestion of a church construction association and under the patronage of the king, the Matthäuskirche was built from 1844–46 and was the first church in Berlin to be built in the centre of a square (a trend followed by many later churches) – although this church was only in the middle of the later Matthäikirchstrasse which was subsequently widened to form a square. The privy councillor district was destroyed during the last few weeks of the Second World War.

Today the Matthäuskirche is the only older building for miles around, but alongside such modern architecture it becomes very apparent just how modern the clear tectonic structure still – or again – appears. Stüler did not simply fall back on the early Christian repertoire of forms; he also shows the building's structure. The three nave aisles each have separate ridge roofs, and the interior sub-division of the piers is shown on the outside by pilaster strips.

The grouping of the round arch windows and the two-storey structure are also characteristic. At the end of the central axis is a slender high tower which has an arcade gallery crowned by four pinnacles and an octagonal top section with a pointed spire. The

chancel was originally designed to consist of a simple apse, but Stüler had to change his plans on the instructions of the king. The interior of the surprisingly large church (which seats 1500) is generous and modern in its design.

Classicism
August Stüler 1844–46
Tiergarten, Matthäikirchplatz (Kulturforum)
Open: Tues–Sun 12–18 hrs., Tel. 262 12 02
www.stiftung-stmatthaeus.de
▷ Bus M29, M41, 148, 200

Hamburger Bahnhof (Hamburg Station)

The last surviving railway station of the first generation in Berlin owes its survival to strange circumstances. It was used as a museum from 1906 onwards, and after the Second World War it was situated in West Berlin – but because it was former railway property it came under the administration of the East Berlin "Reichsbahn". But they were not able or willing to do anything with it – according to the treaties between the Allies, their rights in the western part of the city were restricted to transport tasks. Thus the former station was in a sort of hibernation for 40 years before it came under the West Berlin Senate in 1984 as part of the transfer of the S-Bahn urban railway system. This was a typical curiosity in postwar Berlin, but it was a stroke of good luck for the building.

In 1841, the construction of a railway line between the two largest German cities, Hamburg and Berlin, was agreed in a state treaty. In 1846, the first trip to Hamburg began in a goods shed in Berlin because the station was still under construction. The work was fraught with technical problems: the marshy land had to be filled in with sand, and to do so the Spree canal was diverted to the north. To link the new rail network to the waterways, the Spandau shipping canal and Humboldthafen were built at the same time and completed in 1859.

Construction work on the station itself took only one year and ended in 1847. The main facade crowned by two towers, in which the central section appears like a city gate, is unmistakably classical. But behind it was a sensational architectural innovation: a station hall of iron and glass with four rail lines. The left hand western line was for arrivals, the right hand line for departures and the two middle lines were used for shunting. All four rails led through the two large arches, the present entrance portal, to an outer yard with a large turntable for the locomotives. The passenger service facilities were in the side wings, and the entrances to the two sections of the station were at the front.

In 1874 the turntable was removed and the gates were glazed. In 1877 the platform hall was extended by 53 metres, but even that was insufficient to cope with the extreme increase in the number of passengers. In 1884, only 37 years after it was opened, the station was closed down.

In 1906 the museum of transport and building was established, and from 1911 to 1916 two wings were added on the street side, thus creating the present court of honour.

The alterations for the Museum of Contemporary Art, which opened in 1966, were designed by Josef Paul Kleihues. He also created the 80 metre long extension to the right of the main hall.

Classicism
Friedrich Neuhaus, Ferdinand Wilhelm Holz 1846 / 47; alterations and extension by Josef Paul Kleihues 1990–96
Tiergarten, Invalidenstrasse 50–51
Open: Tues–Fri 10–18 hrs., Sat–Sun 11–18 hrs., Tel. 39 78 34 39
www.smb.museum
▷ S / U Hauptbahnhof

Neue Synagoge (New Synagogue)

140 years ago in one of the first architectural competitions in Berlin, there were already problems with jury decisions. Because the jury was unable to agree on a prizewinner, the jury chairman simply took over the project himself. Eduard Knoblauch had set up as a private architect in 1830 in view of the dominant position of Schinkel in the state building sector – and he was the first successful private architect. The synagogue was his greatest work – and his last building. After he was taken ill, the construction supervision was taken over by his friend August Stüler.

There had been Jews in Berlin since the Middle Ages, although they had often been persecuted and in the 16th century even expelled from the city for a time. The Jewish community was officially founded in 1671, but it was only in the 19th century that Jews were given equal rights with Christians. From that time the Jewish community grew rapidly, and as a result plans were made for a large main synagogue which would seat 3000 and be the largest in Europe.

During the "Reichskristallnacht" the synagogue was rescued by a spirited policeman and the fire brigade, but it was destroyed by bombs in 1943. The ruins of the large synagogue were cleared in 1970, and the front building was restored in the 1990s.

The facade is aligned with the other buildings on the street and dominated by the majestic dome which rests on a tambour and bears a Moorish gold-plated, ribbed lattice. The entrance wall is set back from two tower structures, the top of which corresponds to the main dome.

The facade is horizontally structured by coloured bands of bricks and has oriental motifs; the entrance arcades are exact replicas of motifs of the Alhambra.

The upper women's balcony was once reached via the two side entrances. The three central portals lead into the round vestibule, which Knoblauch skilfully used to compensate for the axis of the

plot which twists to the right. It led into the rectangular anteroom with wardrobe, the small synagogue for daily services and finally the longer rectangular main synagogue. The ceiling structure here was in five parts; iron beams bore the side galleries and the covering arches. Above that are further arches, and above the central aisle are domes.

Today the old building, which is used for various exhibitions, is linked with the adjacent new building of the Centrum Judaicum to its right.

Late classicism
Eduard Knoblauch, August Stüler 1860–66
Mitte, Oranienburger Strasse 28–30
Open: Sun–Thurs 10–18 hrs., Fri 10–14 hrs., Tel. 88 02 83 00
www.cjudaicum.de
▷ S Oranienburger Strasse, tram M1, M6

Rotes Rathaus (Red Town Hall)

The red town hall, so called because of the colour of the building material, was the seat of the city government from 1869 – and has been used for this purpose for the whole of Berlin since 1991. It replaced the mediaeval town hall, which was situated at its north-western corner and which had over the centuries become a mixture of various building elements as a result of fires and alterations and was unable to meet the functional requirements. But it was only in the 1850s that the city, which had repeatedly been limited in its municipal independence by the Electors and kings, decided to build a new town hall. In 1860 the task was given to Hermann Friedrich Waesemann, a former assistant of Stüler and a member of the ministerial building commission.

An entire district of the city had to be demolished to make way for the new building with its ground area of 99 by 88 metres. To the outside it appears as a four wing building, but in the interior there are intermediate wings which create three inner courtyards.

The block-type appearance and the tall, broad-topped tower of Waesemann's design follow the town hall architecture of the formerly powerful cities of Italy and Flanders. With its neo-Renaissance elements, and in spite of the prominent round arches, the town hall is clearly set apart from post-Schinkel classicism, thus establishing a separate municipal architectural style that was distinct from the royal buildings.

The building is impressive with its even rows of round arch openings. The four storeys, of which the middle two are visually linked by the tall window frames, are crowned by an overhanging console balustrade which links the pronounced corner projections to create a fortress-type appearance. But the dominant feature is the 74 metre high tower which rises above the central projection with the high portal. The motif of corner structures supported by thick columns is similar to the cathedral towers of Laon and Naumburg. The surrounding terracotta frieze consists of 36 panels showing

the history of Berlin up to 1871. Most interior rooms were renovated in a modern style after the war.

When this generously sized building nevertheless became too small, the "Stadthaus" (1902–11) was built at the rear of the red town hall. In its design, Ludwig Hoffmann followed the form of the domed churches on Gendarmenmarkt. The complex follows the old street pattern and describes a trapezoidal ground layout around four inner courtyards. Originally, a high mansard roof made the dense facade with its 101 metre high tower appear even more solid. During the GDR period the building was used by the government (Council of Ministers), and it is now again used by the Berlin Senate.

Historicism
Hermann Friedrich Waesemann 1861–69
Mitte, Rathausstrasse 15
▷ S / U Alexanderplatz

Alte Nationalgalerie (Old National Gallery)

The plan developed by Friedrich Wilhelm IV. and Stüler also included a festival hall for the university. Stüler designed an antique
temple building on a high pedestal with a double outdoor flight
of steps in front. The building was particularly designed for the
distant views at the north-east of the Spree island. The basement
was to contain lecture rooms, but the project was never implemented. It was only in 1861, when the banker Wagener bequeath-
ed his collection to the state on condition that a national gallery
be built, that Stüler's design was reconsidered. The building was
not ideal for museum purposes, but its exposed position and its
height guaranteed sufficient light. After Stüler died, the building
work was supervised from 1866–76 by Heinrich Strack, who also
designed the interior.

The building is a temple of the Corinthian order which ends in a
semi-circle at the rear. Eight columns at the front form a portico
with a gable; on the sides the building has half-columns, and on
the wall between them are panels with the names of German
artists. The rear wall of the portico bears a frieze which portrays
the history of the development of German art – from Charlemagne
to Kaulbach – and the gable relief, "Germania as the Protectress
of the Arts." The three female figures on the gable peak personify
painting, sculpture and architecture. The outdoor flight of steps is
purely for representation purposes, as the entrance is at the bottom of the steps. Above it is an equestrian statue of Friedrich Wilhelm IV. by Alexander Calandrelli. On special occasions fires once
burned in the bowls at the base of the balustrade.

The 12-metre-high pedestal contains a storage and administrative floor and a storey that was originally designed for sculptures.
The upper, column-faced part of the building has three high rooms
in the centre which are lit by daylight through skylights, and
around these rooms are two further exhibition storeys.

In 1935 the large halls were divided up into two floors. Towards

the Spree and the street the complex is separated from the every-day hustle and bustle by a series of colonnades. The National Gallery was completely restored in 1996–2001 according to plans drawn up by the Stuttgart architects HG Merz.

Classicism
August Stüler, Heinrich Strack 1866–76
Mitte, Bodestrasse (museum island)
Open: Tues–Sun 10–18 hrs., Thurs 10–22 hrs., Tel. 20 90 55 77
www.smb.museum
▷ S Hackescher Markt, bus 100

Postfuhramt (Postal Stagecoach Building)

Three large buildings dominate the appearance of Oranienburger Strasse. Two of them – the new synagogue and the Tacheles – are well known, but the third building is still in a state of obscurity. Few people know its name or its history – and yet it is one of the most impressive historic buildings in Berlin, and perhaps the most elaborate building of the period for a public service authority. The former postal stagecoach building on the corner of Tucholskystrasse was built from 1875–81 according to plans by Carl Schwatlo. There was an earlier postilion building on the site as early as the beginning of the 18th century.

Behind the two-winged main building are two lower court wings, and it was the former use of these structures which gave the name to the whole complex: the stagecoach halls with stables for about 250 horses. The main building contained the administrative offices, apartments for post office employees, a post office and a telegraph engineers' office. A further building in the courtyard served as the machine and boiler house for the Berlin pneumatic tube conveyor system.

The dominant element of the three-storey brick building is the oblique corner section which is framed between two-axis facade projections. It opens up into a monumental round arch recess spanning three storeys. Above this corner element is an octagonal tambour with a flat dome, with two smaller tambour domes above the facade projections.

The wall facades of the two long facades are structured by bands of facing bricks. The windows, friezes, console balustrade, pilasters and the panels between the windows are adorned with terracotta decorations.

On Tucholskystrasse the building joins onto an extension with a large meeting hall which is marked off externally as a projection with an attic and two groups of figures.

The former postal stagecoach building was used until 1995 by the

German postal service, after which it stood empty for years. But thanks to C / O Berlin, the "International Forum for Visual Dialogues," it has been one of Berlin's most exciting exhibition and event venues for several years now. The cupola hall is used by the Rodeo Club and Restaurent. The building's future, however, is unclear. There have already been several rumors that it is to be sold to investors.

Nearby, on the opposite side of the street, are other postal service buildings: The former main telegraph office at Oranienburger Strasse 73–76 and Monbijoustrasse dates from 1910–13, the former telephone office at Tucholskystrasse 6–14, with its vertically structured facing brick facade, was built in 1925 / 26. The oldest building on the street is integrated into the complex – the former Great National Lodge of Germany which was built in 1789–91 by Christian Becherer.

Historicism
Carl Schwatlo 1875–81
Oranienburger Strasse 35–36 / corner of Tucholskystrasse
www.co-berlin.de
▷ S Oranienburger Strasse, tram M1, M6

Martin-Gropius-Bau (Martin Gropius Building)

Whereas most museum buildings are named after their sponsors or founders such as Guggenheim, Wallfraf-Richartz and Ludwig, the former Museum of Arts and Crafts bears the name of its architect, probably because it no longer contains a permanent exhibition, at least in the main exhibition area. Gropius, a great-uncle of the famous Bauhaus architect Walter Gropius, founded the company of Gropius & Schmieden with his partner Heino Schmieden and became one of the first successful private architects, with numerous villas and hospital buildings. With his strict formal language, he was one of the last proponents of Schinkel classicism.

The basic form of the building, which was built in 1877–81, was based on Schinkel's building academy which was demolished in 1961 – an almost square three-storey, four-wing brick building around a glass-covered inner courtyard. However, the sandstone surrounds of the typical Schinkel three-section windows, the individual decorations and the protruding roof are influenced by the Italian Renaissance and show that even Gropius was not able to resist the influence of the prevalent style of Historicism.

The elevation is sub-divided into a granite pedestal, two evenly designed main storeys and a top storey marked off by a frieze with mosaic and terracotta panels between the windows showing references to the various branches and eras of arts and crafts. The building is crowned by a protruding roof ledge.

The main entrance, designed as a distinguished entrance facade, is located on the northern side. However, as the Berlin Wall was just a few metres away, the entrance was moved to the south in the reconstruction of 1979–81, and the main staircase on the southern side is the only structure projecting out of the rectangular building. Following another revision, the visitor of today is led through the large vestibule into the glass-covered courtyard and from there enters the three storey exhibition area.

Since it was re-opened in 1981, the Martin Gropius building has mainly been used for special exhibitions.

To the north of the Gropius building, and in the east of the city until 1989, is the former Prussian parliament building, now the seat of the Berlin city parliament, which was built in 1892–97 by Friedrich Schulze.

Late classicism
Martin Gropius and Heino Schmieden 1877–81
Kreuzberg, Niederkirchnerstrasse 7, corner of Stresemannstrasse 110
Open: Weds–Mon 10–20 hrs., Tel. 25 48 60
www.gropiusbau.de
▷ S / U Potsdamer Platz, S Anhalter Bahnhof

S-Bahnhof Hackescher Markt
(Hackescher Markt Urban Railway Station)

In 1882, building a railway through the inner city was a completely revolutionary idea in Europe. Four decades had passed since the first Berlin rail link had opened (to Potsdam, 1838), and from 1878 ten routes led away from the capital of the Reich in all the directions of the compass. A ring of nine terminal stations surrounded the inner city. In 1867–77 the circular railway had been built to connect these long-distance railway lines in a large circle (of 37 kilometres) around the city.

But to connect the city centre to the long-distance railway routes and the circular line, work began in 1875 on the "city railway" which was to pass through the length of Berlin from east to west. In order to avoid hindering road traffic, the 12 kilometre section from Schlesischer Bahnhof to Charlottenburg was built above street level – mainly as a viaduct on a total of 731 brick arches. The remaining sections to Westkreuz and Ostkreuz were constructed on embankments.

Four rails were laid, two for local traffic and two for long-distance trains which stopped at five stations: Charlottenburg, Zoologischer Garten, Friedrichstrasse, Alexanderplatz and Schlesischer Bahnhof. The first train travelled the route in 1882 with Emperor Wilhelm I. as the guest of honour.

Until the recent renovation work, only one station building remained almost in its original condition: the urban railway station at Hackescher Markt, formerly known as "Börse". The hall, measuring 100 metres in length and 16 metres in width, has a low-arched roof and originally had a steep skylight in the middle. The side facing Hackescher Markt is richly decorated; cascading low arches rise above the lower shops, and the upper storey with its round windows framed by two projecting elements and the side ornamentation panels reflect Renaissance elements.

Unfortunately, the interior has been unhistorically "historicised". Neither the tiles nor the lamps correspond to the original condition.

Incidentally, the same also applies to all of the stations of the old city railway that have now been renovated.

Even the two stations at Alexanderplatz and Friedrichstrasse were recently stripped down to their skeleton in the 1990s, and the historical Lehrter Stadtbahnhof made way for the new Central Train Station. Another station which has already been fundamentally altered in its interior is Bahnhof Zoo, a bold steel and glass structure built in 1934–36 for the Olympic Games.

Historicism
Johannes Vollmer 1878–82
Mitte, Hackescher Markt
▷ S Hackescher Markt, tram M1, M2, M4, M5, M6

Markthalle VI /Ackerhalle (Market Hall VI)

A little-known but remarkable feature in Berlin's architectural history consists of the municipal market halls dating from the end of the 19th century, four of which are preserved in their original condition or are being restored.

The market halls were an improvement: for the residents next to the old weekly markets they eliminated a source of smell and noise, and the customers and traders could now conduct their business out of the weather and in a more structured fashion.

But the first market hall in Berlin, which opened on Schiffbauer-damm in 1867 under private ownership, was a financial failure. It had to close again after only six months. The Schuman circus moved into the building, it later became Max Reinhardt's great playhouse and was rebuilt after the Second World War as the Friedrichstadtpalast.

The first municipal market hall only opened in 1886, and within the next seven years a central market hall was built on Alexander-platz and extended by a second hall soon afterwards, and 13 market halls were built in various suburbs and numbered in chro-nological order with Roman numerals.

The person responsible for building all the market halls was the municipal building councillor Hermann Blankenstein, and the brick-faced facades are similar in appearance, with their terracotta decorative elements which are sometimes elaborate but always restrained.

Market hall VI in Ackerstrasse is the only one of the four old halls which still have the original exterior. Like all the halls it has two en- trances, but whereas they were usually at the ends, here they are in the corners. Most market halls were built in a block residential context so that only two narrow facades had to be financed. Small shops were established next to the entrances, and dwellings for the shop owners were created on the first floor.

All halls were built to a uniform pattern: a high central aisle lit

by side windows leads into traverse side aisles with skylights. The roof is supported by cast-iron girders and steel trusses.

Since its renovation in 1990 / 91, the "Ackerhalle" has contained a supermarket. Opposite is the ruin of the Elisabethkirche by Schinkel, which is worth viewing.

Lively market activity can still be seen in the Arminiushalle in Moabit which, unusually, occupies an entire block. However, the facade facing Arminiusstrasse has been altered, and the same applies to the market halls in Kreuzberg on Eisenbahnstrasse and Marheinekeplatz.

Historicism
Hermann Blankenstein 1888
Mitte, Ackerstrasse 23–26 / Invalidenstrasse 159
Open: Mon–Fri 8–20 hrs., Sat 8–16 hrs.
▷ U Rosenthaler Platz, S Nordbahnhof

Reichstagsgebäude (Reichstag Building)

Ludwig Bohnstedt was the clear winner of the Reichstag competition. But his popular design (with a monumental front symbolic of openness) disappeared into a drawer – the time was evidently not yet ripe for a separate parliamentary building. Ten years later, in 1882, a second competition was declared, and this time the winner was Paul Wallot, a private architect in Frankfurt / Main. But he, too, had to endure quarrels with the Emperor and the authorities before the building was eventually dedicated in 1894.

Construction began in 1884, but the final decision on the facade design was only made in 1886 and as late as 1890, when the interior load-bearing walls were already finished, a new dome had to be designed to suit the will of Wilhelm II.

The eventual result was a four-wing structure with two inner courtyards and with the plenary parliamentary chamber at the centre. The main facade faces west, away from the centre of the city.

Above a rusticated pedestal facade, the monumental structure rises in two storeys. The characteristic features are the protruding square corner towers and the entrance section which also forms a block projecting out of the line of the building. In front of the entrance is a row of columns with a triangular gable and a large outdoor flight of steps leading to the portal. Above the central plenary chamber, a large dome of iron and glass rose from a rectangular base, and it was much admired as a masterpiece of engineering.

At a height of 75 metres on the lantern was an emperor's crown. The exterior was sub-divided by a colossal structure and had rich figure ornamentations around the top. The interior was also luxuriously ornamented.

In the Reichstag fire on 28.2.1933 the interior, and especially the plenary chamber, were partly destroyed. In the last days of the war, the Reichstag suffered severe damage and again burned out. The dome was later detonated for safety reasons.

After long discussions about its future use, the interior of the

building was fitted out in a sober and rational style to plans by Paul Baumgarten, but the plenary chamber remained provisional.

After it was decided that Berlin would be the future seat of government, a competition was declared and the winner was Sir Norman Foster. But the design that was implemented – also by Sir Norman Foster – has nothing in common with the winning design. The interior was completely hollowed out and the plenary chamber, which is again at the centre of the building, is now below an elliptical glass dome on a round base with ramps leading to the top. As from April 1999, the Reichstag building is the official seat of the German parliament.

The neighbouring Reichstag President's Palace was also designed by Wallot (1897–1903).

Historicism
Paul Wallot 1884–94; last alterations by Sir Norman Foster 1994–99
Tiergarten, Platz der Republik
dome: daily 8–24 hrs.
www.bundestag.de
▷ S / U Brandenburger Tor, bus 100

Riehmers Hofgarten (Riehmer's Court Garden)

In 1858–62, in view of the enormous population influx due to the Industrial Revolution, James Hobrecht (an employee at police headquarters) drafted a development plan for the extension of the city which envisaged a generous right-angled grid of streets with wide thoroughfares and a large number of city squares. As a result, Berlin had an urban planning framework which was influential for decades and prevented wild development in the surrounding area but also initiated the development of Berlin as the "largest tenement complex in the world". As the state had to bear the costs of road development, the blocks were generously proportioned: 200 to 400 metres long and 150 to 200 metres deep. There were no regulations for the interior building, merely a building regulation of 1853 which prescribed that a courtyard must be at least 5.30 by 5.30 metres (to enable the firefighting hose to turn), a size which was increased in 1887 to 60 square metres. To maximise profits, the large building plots were densely developed, often with several inner courtyards.

But two examples show that there were also other alternatives besides just linking up one courtyard after another. The master bricklayer Riehmer used his plot in Kreuzberg, which faces onto three streets, to break up the normal rear courtyard structure by adding a private road. By providing a higher residential standard and mainly flats with three or more rooms, he hoped to attract better situated tenants from the civil service or bourgeois classes – and this aim paid off. The garden design increased the attractiveness.

Almost twenty buildings are grouped around the court garden. As with all tenement buildings of the period, the larger flats face the street and the smaller flats face the courtyard. The style of the facade, with its elaborate neo-baroque and Renaissance forms, followed contemporary taste. The impressive facades facing Grossbeerenstrasse and Yorckstrasse are particularly striking,

with two atlantes supporting the lower balcony above the entrance to the court. Other typical Renaissance elements are the thick beams at the top of the facade. On closer inspection, the details of the ornamentation show the different building phases. In the 1970s and 1980s the complex was carefully renovated and the flats were modernised. Today, Riehmer's courtyard garden is a popular residential address. The complex also contains office, doctors' surgeries, restaurants and three cinemas.

A second example of an unconventional block development within Hobrecht's street grid is the town villa estate in a private road on Genthiner Strasse in the district of Tiergarten.

Historicism
O. Moes and W. Riehmer 1891–99
Kreuzberg, Yorckstrasse / Hagelberger Strasse / Grossbeerenstrasse
▷ U Mehringdamm, bus M19

Kurfürstendamm

From early times, rich citizens of Berlin were attracted to the west, first of all to Friedrichstadt, then outside the city gates to the "privy councillor district", and from the end of the 19th century, to the villa districts far beyond the city boundaries. The trend began with Alsen (now Wannsee) from 1864 and Lichterfelde and Westend from 1866. In 1889 the "Kurfürstendamm society" added the grandest residential district: Grunewald. And for those who did not want to go to the green countryside, a magnificent urban residential district arose from the 1890s along Kurfürstendamm in the previously undeveloped area between Charlottenburg and Wilmersdorf.

For centuries the "Ku'damm" was simply a track connecting the Electoral Grunewald hunting palace with the residence. It was only in 1881, at the suggestion of Otto von Bismarck, that it was built up as a 53 metre wide street that he was proud of to the end of his life.

Noble villas were built, especially in the side streets, although very few of them survive today. The loveliest example is the "Wintergarten ensemble" on Fasanenstrasse containing the literature house, the Käthe Kollwitz museum and Villa Grisebach, which was built in the 1890s.

But the villas were soon replaced by high class tenement buildings. The apartments had ten or more rooms including a saloon, a reception room, a library and other necessary rooms, and in some cases they covered an area of 500 square metres or more.

The ground floors also often contained apartments, but cafés, restaurants, cinemas, cabarets, shops and galleries soon followed. The "Ku'damm" became an elegant shopping boulevard and a meeting place for writers and artists. The emblems of the "new west" were the Kaiser Wilhelm memorial church and the "Romanisches Café".

The facades contained a wild mixture of quotations from the history of architecture. The result was a wonderfully bombastic architecture with towers, balconies, bay windows, columns, gables

and ledges, all covered with rich decorations. The interiors were dominated by high ceilings with stucco ornamentation, magnificent house entrances and staircases.

About half of the buildings were lost in the war, and they have been replaced by functional office buildings, thus robbing the "Ku'damm" of its noble character – and even by the frequent thoughtless alterations of the shopping zones.

But it is still possible to find genuine jewels of historical bombasticism along "Ku'damm" and in the side streets, especially between Bleibtreustrasse and Leibnizstrasse. The building in the photograph is on the corner of Kurfürstendamm and Leibnizstrasse.

Even today the area around the "Ku'damm" is residential, especially the rear buildings and upper storeys, even though many offices have now moved into the enormous old apartments.

Historicism / Art Nouveau
Approx. 1890–1910
Charlottenburg, Wilmersdorf, Kurfürstendamm and side streets
▷ U Kurfürstendamm, U Uhlandstrasse, U Adenauerplatz, S Halensee, bus M19, M29, X10, 109, 110

Berliner Dom (Berlin Cathedral)

Although the present building just celebrated its 100th anniversary, the history of the Berlin cathedral reaches back to the Middle Ages. In 1469 a cathedral chapter was founded in the palace chapel, and in 1536 it was moved to the church of the dissolved Dominican monastery to the south of the palace. But this building, which the Elector had selected as the family burial site, fell into disrepair and had to be demolished in 1747. Johann Boumann built a simple church with a tambour dome on the present site, and Schinkel altered it in 1817–22. However, it remained architecturally unsatisfying. As early as 1828, Schinkel himself presented new plans based on the style of an early Christian five-aisled basilica. Work began in 1842 to a design by Stüler and was discontinued in 1848. Then Stüler designed an enormous dome with four towers with a width of 48 metres – but in vain. A competition in 1867 failed because the jury did not consider any of the entries to be appropriate.

It was only in 1888 through Julius Raschdorff, a professor of architecture at the technical university in Charlottenburg, that the matter came to life again. His plan envisaged three central naves alongside each other with tambour domes and an enormous tower. A covered bridge was to link the cathedral to the palace. This design also failed, but the new Emperor Wilhelm II. encouraged Raschdorff to make a new suggestion, and this suggestion was finally implemented in a significantly reduced form – against the objections of the building academy, the cathedral construction committee and the cathedral church college, which criticised it on stylistic, liturgical and acoustic grounds. But the Emperor ignored all criticism and obtained the approval of the regional parliament for a subsidy of 10 million marks. The foundation stone was laid in 1894, and the building was finally dedicated in 1905.

The church measures 114 by 73 metres, the dome is 75 metres high up to the base of the lantern. The building is sub-divided into

the main preaching church and the small baptism and weddings church; the monument church on the northern side was demolished in 1975 / 76. Below the preaching church is a crypt with the coffins of the Hohenzollern family; some sarcophages are displayed in the sermon church. There are numerous auxiliary rooms and staircases.

The main building was heavily damaged in 1944 and could only be used again in 1993. The main dome and the four top tower sections were originally steeper and elaborately decorated.

The cathedral and the Reichstag building are regarded as the main works of "Wilhelm baroque" (although the cathedral is neo-renaissance in its forms). It is exemplary in its excessive size and forms, and a symbol of the Hohenzollerns' religious concept of divine favour.

Historicism
Julius Raschdorff 1894–1905, partly simplified
Mitte, Am Lustgarten
Open: Mon–Sat 9–20 hrs., Sun 12–20 hrs., Tel. 20 26 91 36
www.berliner-dom.de
▷ S Hackescher Markt, bus 100

Theater des Westens (Theatre of the West)

The "Theater des Westens" is a unique architectural structure. The front building with the main facades facing Kantstrasse (the present main entrance) and Fasanenstrasse (the former main entrance) shows a unique mixture of Renaissance, Empire and Art Nouveau elements which are elegant and yet cheerful and vivacious.

Above the rusticated pedestal storey rises the high main storey, which consists of two storeys in the interior, with a colossal order and round arch windows. The glazing bars are interesting in form, giving an impression of perspective. At the top of the facade is an attic crowned with sculptures. The block type corners are impressively topped with roof lanterns. The inscription can be translated as "This building was built for the care of the arts".

The part of the building containing the stage is similar in style to the mediaeval fortress of Eltz: a brick building with battlements, bays, gables, towers and half timber framework. The interior is dominated by plush and pomp.

The architecture thus exactly matches the character of the theatre: it is a site for light entertainment, from 1898 in the form of operettas, and today with musicals. The building was used as the home of the German opera house from 1945–61 and the interior was radically modernised for the purpose, but since 1978 it has again been characterised by the old extravagance.

Berlin also has a small and splendid theatre in the Art Nouveau style: the Hebbel theatre in Kreuzberg which was built in 1907 / 08 by Oskar Kaufmann. The facade cladding with its rough-hewn shell limestone panels, which are usually only used for the pedestal zone of a building, give the building a fortified air. The characteristic feature of the facade is the curved window complex in a wall recess. The intimate interior is particularly impressive with its artistic wooden panelling.

That applies even more to Kaufmann's Renaissance theatre in Hardenbergstrasse (1926 / 27), where the facade does not reflect

the high quality of the interior. A further building by Kaufmann is the impressive Volksbühne building on Rosa-Luxemburg-Platz (1913–15), which was restored in simplified form after the war. Whereas the Deutsches Theater, the Berliner Ensemble and the Komische Oper (in spite of its modern exterior) were built in neo-baroque splendour, the Schillertheater is in the monumental plain form of the 1950s. Both theatres by Fritz Bornemann are modern and functional: the Deutsche Oper (1956–61) and the Freie Volks-bühne (1960–63).

Historicism / Art Nouveau
Bernhard Sehring 1895–96
Charlottenburg, Kantstrasse 12
www.theater-des-westens.de
▷ S / U Zoologischer Garten, U Kurfürstendamm

Stadtgericht Mitte (Mitte Court Building)

The former regional and local court building behind the red town hall was once the second largest building in the city, only surpassed by the palace. Although it was barbarically decimated in 1968, it is still the most interesting of the many splendid court buildings in Berlin – mainly because of its impressive staircase.

The four-storey complex once had a length of 220 metres parallel to the S-Bahn urban railway line. The two long wings were linked by traverse sections, between which there were five large and six smaller open courtyards. In 1968 the northern section on Grunerstrasse was demolished to make way for road widening, and since then the protruding projection on Littenstrasse is no longer in the centre of the facade.

The exterior was greatly simplified during restoration work after the war. Neither the former mansard roof nor the roof decorative elements were reconstructed. The rusticated ground floor is built of hewn stone, and the upper storeys of rendered brick. When these were restored in 2009, however, a new tower was built on each.

Paul Thoemer and Rudolf Mönnich originally designed a typical Wilhelm-type state building in an elaborate neo-baroque style, but the implementing architect Otto Schmalz preferred Art Nouveau, which is clearly reflected in the central element of the facade, and he gave the building its most distinctive feature, the staircase – which is at the same time a reception hall and a "distributor" to the various wings of the building. It consists of a high hall with an elongated ground layout on narrow contoured pillars which support balcony-like galleries. On the long sides, flights of stairs set in opposite directions lead upwards. With its dynamically curved lines in the floor plan and the elevation and its details such as stair rails, floor tiles and stucco ornaments it is a fine example of Art Nouveau. A rather smaller second staircase which was just as elaborate was once by Grunerstrasse, but was sacrificed

to road construction in 1968. Until 1990, the building was used as the supreme court of the GDR.

Other historic "palaces of law" with elaborate staircases can be found in Moabit, Wedding, Charlottenburg and Schöneberg.

In front of the main facade of the court building is the ruin of the Gothic Franciscan church which was built in the second half of the 13th century and, until 1945, was one of the major buildings in Berlin. Close by to the south are the last remains of the old city wall, which was built of boulder and brick at the beginning of the 14th century; in the shade of the ruined wall, a number of small town houses with facades from the 18th century are still preserved.

Historicism / Art Nouveau
Paul Thoemer, Rudolf Mönnich, Otto Schmalz 1896–1904; simplified and reduced in size after the war
Mitte, Littenstrasse 11–17, corner of Grunerstrasse
▷ S / U Alexanderplatz, U Klosterstrasse

Märkisches Museum
(Museum of the Mark Brandenburg)

On the south bank of the Spree just before it divides into two arms, the tower of the museum is one of the most important landmarks in the city.

Although it may seem strange at first sight, the museum complex was built in one single construction period to plans by the Berlin architectural councillor Ludwig Hoffmann, who had won an architectural competition. The competition was declared so that the museum of the Mark Brandenburg, which had been founded in 1874 and provisionally housed in the Palais Podewils since then, would at last have its own building.

The principle applied by Stüler in the 1840s in his interior design for the Neues Museum, i.e. to design the rooms specifically for the exhibits, was now transferred to the exterior by Hoffmann (following Gabriel von Seidl's Bavarian National Museum in Munich). Because the museum of the Mark Brandenburg documented the historical and artistic development of the region through the centuries, Hoffmann created a complex grouped around two inner courtyards with completely different building sections, many of which went back to specific architectural examples in Brandenburg. For example, the tower with its hiproof is based on the keep of the Bischofsburg in Wittstock, the broken gables and the ornamentation of the Gothic facade sections are modelled on the Katharinenkirche in Brandenburg / Havel.

The interior was also designed to match the collections; vaulted corridors and rooms create the atmosphere for mediaeval exhibits. And a number of original architectural elements were integrated, e.g. the monumental brick portal of 1316 from the "Hohes Haus", the mediaeval residence of the margraves in Berlin (Klosterstrasse). Next to the main entrance is a copy of the "Roland" from the town hall in the old part of Brandenburg / Havel.

To the south of the museum is the small Köllnischer Park in which two specimens of Berlin's emblem, the bear, live – separated

from visitors by a deep ditch. Around them, architectural parts and fragments from the architectural history of Berlin can be seen.

In the direct vicinity of the Märkisches Museum, three interesting modern buildings can be seen: the insurance building built in 1903 / 04 by Alfred Messel (Am Köllnischen Park 3), the Expressionist facade of the former AOK health insurance headquarters in Berlin with a length of over 100 metres built by Albert Gottheimer in 1930 / 31 (Rungestrasse 3–6), and especially the trades union building by Max Taut and Franz Hoffmann of 1922 / 23 (Wallstrasse 61–65), the first building in which the (reinforced concrete) frame structure became the dominant element in the facade.

Historicism
Ludwig Hoffmann 1901–07
Mitte, Am Köllnischen Park 5
Open: daily 10–18 hrs., Weds 12–20 hrs., Tel. 24 00 21 62
www.stadtmuseum.de
▷ U Märkisches Museum, S / U Jannowitzbrücke

Deutsche Staatsbibliothek
(German State Library) Unter den Linden

When the old library building in the "Forum Fridericianum" became too small for the collection of the Prussian state library (the former royal library), Emperor Wilhelm II. had the academy building of 1743 pulled down, and an imposing new building by Ernst Ihne was built from 1903–14. The building measures 170 by 106 metres and has an impressive neo-baroque facade. Above a rusticated pedestal storey there are two main storeys combined visually by decorative recesses which enclose the windows of the inter-mediate storey. The roof is concealed by an attic balustrade, and the three-axis central projection facing Unter den Linden is marked out as the entrance by colossal half columns. The entrance to the library is through a courtyard with ivy.

War damage robbed the building of its centre: the reading room with an enormous dome (38 metres in diameter). Today, the spaces for reading are distributed between several smaller rooms. The dome-covered room was first replaced by two storage towers of 13 storeys. These have been torn down by now and a new central reading room with a glass cube of many levels planned by the architect hg. Merz is to be completed by 2011.

The complex includes part of the state library, the library of the Humboldt University at the rear and, in the front wings on Unter den Linden, the Academy of Science.

The state library is a good example of the representation style with which the Emperor wished to present the new self-awareness that had been gained with the foundation of the Reich. Where there had initially been attempts to enliven the classicism of the Schinkel school with Renaissance forms (Martin Gropius building, cf. p. 88f.), they were soon overwhelmed by the trend towards livelier facades which came from Paris. Increasingly bombastic Renaissance and baroque forms with colossal columns, domes, tower tops etc. dominated not only the facades of public buildings, but soon also the street scene in residential districts.

This trend was delayed by the urban building councillors who spent many years in office: Hartmann Blankenstein (1872–96) and Ludwig Hoffmann (1896–1925); the former was sober and conservative in spirit and adhered to late classicism, the latter – with his open-minded eclecticism influenced by Art Nouveau – mediated a link to Modernism. Both have left their mark on the urban setting with their numerous school and administrative buildings.

However it was Ernst Ihne, who was trained in Paris, appointed as the imperial court architect in 1888 and knighted in 1906, who became the dominant architect of "Wilhelm baroque" with the state library, the Bode-Museum, the Neuer Marstall and other buildings.

Historicism
Ernst Ihne 1903–14
Mitte, Unter den Linden 8
▷ U Französische Strasse, S / U Friedrichstrasse

Bode-Museum (Bode Museum) and Pergamonmuseum (Pergamon Museum)

21 years had passed since the opening of the national gallery in 1876 before the next foundation stone was laid on the museum island. There had, in fact, been an architectural competition as early as 1882, but the results were considered inadequate. Finally Ernst Ihne was commissioned to design the Emperor Friedrich Museum, now known as the Bode-Museum (photo). The neo-baroque building is majestically reflected in the water of the two arms of the Spree at the point where they re-unite. The dome, which is above a hall of honour in the interior, is at its most dominant in this exposed position. The entrance is in the rounded end of the building and is reached via the two bridges. The three-wing exterior is much more complex in the interior and has a total of five open courtyards. The renovation of the Bode-Museum was completed in 2005.

The last building on the museum island is the Pergamonmuseum built from 1912–30. Because of the rapid expansion of the collection of works from antiquity, it had to occupy the whole area between the Neues Museum, the national gallery and the S-Bahn urban railway, and it needed high rooms with skylights. The plans were designed by Alfred Messel who had become famous for his department store architecture (Wertheim on Leipziger Platz and on Rosenthaler Strasse, partly still preserved), but he died before construction began. Thus the work began in 1912 under the direction of his friend from youth, Ludwig Hoffmann, but construction dragged on until 1930 and still remained unfinished. In addition to the existing three wing complex it was planned to build a colonnade between the side wings on Kupfergraben, a single storey extension to the Neues Museum along the water (which is at present also part of the plans for the restoration of the Neues Museum), an entrance hall (the present glass box dates from 1982) and a wing linking it to the Bode-Museum, which is cut off from the rest of the island by the railway line. In addition, it was planned to reorganise the urban structure of the area opposite the

main frontage and to create a link from there to Hegelplatz in front of the university.

Colossal Doric pilasters sub-divide the side wings, and on the ends the gables are supported by half-columns. Hoffmann adapted Messel's heavy "state baroque" to classical forms which create a transition to the architectural language of the Neues Museum and Altes Museum. The windowless tall central structure and the large wall surface of the side wings give the complex a rather massive appearance. Since 2008 the museum has been undergoing reconstruction according to plans designed by Oswald Mathias Ungers. In the future the Court of Honour will be accessed via an elevated glass wing located along the Spree.

Historicism with modern elements
Bode-Museum: Ernst Ihne 1897–1904; Pergamonmuseum: Alfred Messel, Ludwig Hoffmann 1912–30
Mitte, Kupfergraben (museum island)
Open: daily 10–18 hrs., Tues 10–22 hrs., Tel. 20 90 55 77
www.smb.museum
▷ S Hackescher Markt, S / U Friedrichstrasse, bus 100

Hackesche Höfe

Outside the so-called Spandau Gate, the densely populated outer suburb "Spandauer Vorstadt" developed by about 1700 and had its own church, the Sophienkirche, from 1712. In 1732–34 Friedrich Wilhelm I. had a new city wall built around the greatly extended urban area, and the former outer suburbs became urban districts. The old fortifications disappeared, and outside Spandau Gate the city commander, Count von Hacke, had a market built.

A large number of Jews subsequently settled in this area, especially from the East. Not far from the Hackescher Markt the first synagogue in Berlin was dedicated in 1714, and the first Jewish cemetery was created on Grosse Hamburger Strasse. The actual Jewish quarter in Berlin was the so-called "Scheunenviertel" (barn district) in the east of the Spandauer Vorstadt. When they became wealthy, many Jews moved west towards Oranienburger Strasse, where the new synagogue was built in 1866. As a result, the term "Scheunenviertel" later denoted the entire Spandauer Vorstadt.

When the district prospered around 1900 and became a respectable address, a man named Quilitz acquired the plot at Rosenthaler Strasse 40/41 and Sophienstrasse 6, had the buildings pulled down and a complex with eight courtyards built – the largest in Europe. Restaurants, industry, shops and flats were built – a colourful mixture it was easy to find tenants for.

The first courtyard was designed by August Endell, who made it a prime example of Art Nouveau. He also created two festive rooms for the Neumann wine tavern, although only one survived and is now used by the Chamäleon variety theatre. In the rear part of the Restaurant Hackescher Hof, the original ceiling is preserved.

The Hackesche Höfe really did become a colourful mix. The tenants were merchants, factory owners, civil servants, restaurant owners and even a choirmaster. In 1916 the Jewish girls' club moved in, and the last owner before the war was the Jewish merchant Jacob Michael.

The Hackesche Höfe were renovated in the nineties and are one of the liveliest settings in Berlin – by day and by night. Whereas the courtyards have been faithfully restored in their original form, the facade facing Hackescher Markt has been modernised. Especially the large round arch in the upper part of the facade is neither original, nor did it exist in the years before the renovation work.

Opposite the complex, the "Neuer Hackescher Markt" has been built, a complex of nine front buildings and three rear buildings, on the basis of a master plan by the Berlin architects Götz Bellmann and Walter Böhm (the individual buildings were designed by a total of four different architectural offices). The different facades with their "modern interpretations of historical building details" and the characteristic roof zones give the Hackescher Markt a striking and lively atmosphere.

Historicism / Art Nouveau
1905–07 Kurt Berndt, August Endell; facade altered
Mitte, Hackescher Markt
www.hackeschehoefe.de
▷ S Hackescher Markt

U-Bahnhof Wittenbergplatz
(Wittenbergplatz Underground Station)

The "disfigurement of Wittenbergplatz and the surrounding area by the high station building" was a major topic in the media in 1913. The controversy was caused by the 15 metre high ticket hall building "by which the residents of Kleiststrasse suffer severe loss in their material circumstances" and which "because of its size has become an obstacle between Tauentzienstrasse and Kleiststrasse and separated them, making them effectively dead-end roads".

How times change! The long-neglected building was made a protected monument in 1980 (against the will of the BVG transport company) and restored to its former glory (albeit in simplified form) in 1983, and since then it has been regarded as a jewel of the western city centre of Berlin, which is not rich in architectural treasures.

Alfred Grenader, who was the company architect of the overground and underground railway from 1899 to 1931, designed a cross-shaped entrance and ticket hall with neo-classical forms and a square tower block. It also serves as a junction of three platforms with five rail lines – the sixth one was not built, which made the station asymmetrical. The steel framework structure is faced with shell sandstone slabs.

Berlin could easily have been the first city in Europe with an U-Bahn (underground railway) system. As early as 1867, Werner Siemens had developed the first plans for an electrical overground railway. But the resistance from the authorities and the general public was enormous. The royal permit to build the first Berlin overground railway was only issued in 1893, and the route was to be built and operated by Siemens, and was to be in the south of the city – to supplement the S-Bahn to the north, and out of the way where it would not disturb people. It was opened in 1902. In the city of Berlin it was built on stilts, but the town of Charlottenburg insisted on a "rail below the streets", so from the

beginning it disappeared underground at the former city boundary between Nollendorfplatz and Wittenbergplatz.

The overground stations of the route U1 in Kreuzberg and Schöneberg have a major effect on the urban setting. Structures which are particularly worth viewing include the Oberbaumbrücke (1894–96 by Otto Stahn), Schlesisches Tor station, the only solid brick building with an attractive and rich stylistic exterior which does not look like an overground station (Grisebach and Dinklage 1899–1901), Görlitz station, which even today retains its original appearance as the standard type, and Kottbusser Tor station, a spacious structure built in 1928–29 by Grenader.

Historicism
Alfred Grenader 1910–13
Schöneberg, Wittenbergplatz
▷ U Wittenbergplatz

AEG-Turbinenhalle (AEG Turbine Hall)

"If you come to Berlin, don't forget to look at the AEG turbine building by Peter Behrens. You just have to see it!" wrote the young Erich Mendelsohn in 1914. The innovative character of this building only becomes clear if we consider the previous situation. Small industrial buildings were often designed by master builders or master masons who are now forgotten, and large buildings and production halls were designed by construction engineers. They engaged architects, if possible famous architects, to design the facade. Thus Franz Schwechten, the architect of the Kaiser Wilhelm memorial church and Anhalter station, designed the facades for the AEG buildings in Ackerstrasse and Brunnenstrasse. But that was not industrial architecture in any real sense – typically for the time, the facades were merely incidental additions without any reference to the function of the building, and the forms of the facades could be applied to any construction task.

In 1907 Emil Rathenau appointed Peter Behrens, who had originally trained as a painter, as the artistic consultant to AEG with responsibility for the overall visual presentation of the company. Behrens, who worked with such people as Gropius, Mies van der Rohe and Le Corbusier, not only designed a new "corporate identity" and supervised the design of all AEG products – with the turbine hall in Moabit in 1909 he also created a model for modern industrial architecture.

For the first time ever, the outer facade of an industrial building showed the bare structure: the steel trusses and their joints are plainly seen outside the glass facade which leans slightly inwards, following the interior supports. The gable of the end wall, in describing six sides of a polygon, also follows the interior structure. But here it is also clear that Behrens did not merely wish to show the structural elements for their own sake. The gable appears to rest on the glass front and the principle of loads and supports appears reversed by the receding ashlar corner pillars. The solid

corner pylons, which are not necessary from a structural point of view, give the facade a solid heaviness which was designed to strengthen the confidence of the workers and the public at large. The architecture in itself became an advertising medium.

The revolutionary character of Behrens' building, which made such an impression on his contemporaries, only becomes clear when it is compared with the "classical" facades with their columns, triangular gables and neo-baroque ornamentation – although later architects criticised the design of the end facade, suggesting that it made too many allowances for tradition.

The hall was originally 110 metres long. In 1939 it was extended to over 200 metres – with architecture of a far weaker character. On the side facing the factory premises it is joined to a further two-storey hall which is faced with hewn stone.

Classical Modernism (Functionalism)
Peter Behrens 1909
Tiergarten (Moabit), Huttenstrasse 12–19
▷ U Turmstrasse, bus M27, 126

Werksanlagen Siemensstadt
(Siemensstadt Factory Complex)

Siemensstadt was the only part of Berlin where a self-contained industrial suburb developed with factory premises, residential areas and supply facilities. Its appearance was particularly influenced by one man: Hans Hertlein, the director of the company's own building department from 1915–51, who created a uniform design not only for the works buildings, but also for the entire suburb. Hertlein's first "modern" building was the works building "Werner-werk M", built from 1917–22. He based his work on the architectural plan of his predecessor Karl Janisch, who built around the edge of the block, but he eliminated all ornamentation. A structural clarity of design replaced the "representation facade".

Originally, the five-storey complex was to enclose twelve inner courtyards, but only three were implemented. The building was destroyed in the war and restored in simplified form. It is dominated by the 70 metre high tower which conceals a chimney for the integrated heating station and a water tank. With its large clock it rises above Siemensstadt like the town halls rose above the then independent communities of Greater Berlin. The idea of a works tower was followed a few years later by Eugen Schmohl for Borsig in Tegel and for Ullstein in Tempelhof.

Hertlein found revolutionary new forms for the switching centre tower block which was built in 1926–28 (photo). In a departure from the strict block pattern, he built a slab-like north-to-south building which is 175 metres long, 16 metres wide and 45 metres high. The building is a steel frame structure in which the outer walls were filled in with bricks and clad with facing bricks. The ten storeys have no supports in the interior, which means that the rooms can be flexibly sub-divided to suit the procedures and requirements within the company. The staircases (with waste disposal facilities) are outside the core building, and in their solid block-type structure they appear as a vertical counterweight to the elongated tall block building. The facade is without any orna-

mentation and is only sub-divided by the exterior supports – a known design element which is here magnified to monumental proportions.

The same applies to Hertlein's Wernerwerk tower building (1928–30). Whereas Wernerwerk M and the switching station tower are in the middle of the factory complex, the Wernerwerk tower block is more accessible because it is situated directly on Siemensdamm.

Hertlein's concept of space-saving production facilities was not followed through. Instead, we now have extensive industrial complexes with windowless boxes without any claim to artistic value.

Classical Modernism (Functionalism / New Rationality)
Hans Hertlein, from 1915
Spandau, Wernerwerk M: Wernerwerkdamm 1–4; switching station tower: Nonnendamm 101–110 behind the main administration; Wernerwerk tower: Siemensdamm 50–55
▷ U Rohrdamm, U Siemensdamm

Mossehaus (Mosse Building)

One building made Erich Mendelsohn in 1920 world-famous at the age of 33: the Einstein tower in Potsdam, which was acclaimed as "Expressionism in perfection" and is still unique today. Mendelsohn was then deluged with commissions, and for many years he directed the largest architectural office in Germany with a staff of over 40. In 1921–23 he created another building which had a revolutionary impact: the Mossehaus.

The printing and editorial building of the Berliner Tageblatt published by Rudolf Mosse was originally built in 1900–03 by Cremer and Wolffenstein as a sandstone building in neo-baroque forms with Art Nouveau elements. When the entrance on the corner was destroyed in street fighting soon after the First World War, Mosse commissioned Erich Mendelsohn to replace the entrance corner and, at the same time, to add two extra storeys in height.

Mendelsohn interrupted the facade completely and inserted a building section with an extreme horizontal orientation of completely different materials (iron and ceramics) into the old building, which he left unchanged. A massive ledge forms a roof over the entrance, above this ledge wide horizontal window bands are arranged one over the other, and in the upper storeys they extend over the entire length of the building. The corner section is emphasised further by an extra top storey. The building, and especially the corner, have a breathtaking dynamism.

"Out of the old facade, almost exploding it, rises the dynamism of the new age", wrote a contemporary architecture critic, who interpreted the Mossehaus as "a monument to the struggling battles of our times".

Erich Mendelsohn was regarded as the ultimate big city architect. Without restriction he affirmed the metropolis with its traffic, its pace and movement, its masses of people and especially its artificial light. He saw it as a complex organism, with corners and

cross-roads as its joints. The middle of the facade was no longer the focal part of the building – instead, he emphasised the corners which extended into the traffic space and gave it direction. The building became part of its environment, and actually played an active role.

The most expressive form for Mendelsohn was the horizontal. In his famous shops in Stuttgart and Chemnitz and the Columbus building on Potsdamer Platz in Berlin, which was pulled down after the war, he used long horizontal window bands and protruding glass staircases to create magnificent and frequently copied facade solutions which were particularly impressive at night when fully illuminated.

Classical Modernism (Expressionism)
Erich Mendelsohn 1921–23; on an old building by Cremer and Wolffenstein 1900–03
Mitte, Schützenstrasse 25
▷ U Spittelmarkt

Borsigturm (Borsig Tower)

It was only in 1922 that Berlin acquired its first skyscraper – far from the city centre in the factory complex of the Borsigwerke in Tegel. The tower still stands as one of the last relics of a bygone industrial age. Most of the buildings around it have been pulled down, and new architecture has only partly filled the waste areas again.

Originally, it was the cramped conditions on the factory complex that led to the construction of the tower – the ground area of the 65 metre high tower is merely 20 by 16 metres.

The tower soon became the symbol of the Borsigwerke which August Borsig had founded outside the Oranienburg gate in 1827 and which within a few decades became the largest locomotive manufacturer in Europe. In 1894 / 95 the company moved into the new factory complex in Tegel, which was gradually extended. The company, which was managed as a family corporation, did not survive the economic crisis of 1929. After several changes of ownership the Borsig company still exists today, but it no longer occupies the factory premises in Tegel.

The tower was built as a steel frame building with brick facades. The staircase is fitted externally to the south side. In the interior, the structure is supported by six vertical members, so that the floor space on each storey can be flexibly sub-divided, ranging from an open plan office to six rooms of almost equal size. Above the base of the building, thick ledges divide the building into three sections of three storeys each. The windows are arranged in groups of three and separated by lesenes. And on top of this calmly structured facade of regular vertical and horizontal elements rises an angular Expressionist upper section which contains the festive hall. Above the high, narrow round arch windows there are facing arches. The tower is crowned by a further small top section.

The architect of this first skyscraper in Berlin was Eugen Schmohl, who also designed the Ullsteinhaus in Tempelhof soon afterwards –

which also had a tower. The model was probably the tower of the Wernerwerk in Siemensstadt built by Hans Hertlein after 1917 (cf. p. 118f.), but naturally there were also many American models. By contrast with the towers of the Wernerwerk and the Ullstein complex, the Borsig tower actually contains offices and is not just an impressive facade for chimneys and water tanks. This tower was also the first example of the use of Expressionist forms in industrial architecture in Berlin.

The Borsig tower was renovated in the 1970s and is now used as an office building. The interior is not accessible to visitors.

On the basis of an urban development concept by Claudio Vasconi a hotel, office buildings and a business founders' centre have been built around the Borsig tower since 1996. The main attraction of the Borsig complex are the old factory halls which have been made into a shopping arcade.

Classical Modernism (Expressionism)
Eugen Schmohl 1922–24
Reinickendorf (Tegel), Berliner Strasse 27
▷ U Borsigwerke

Funkturm (Radio Tower) and Messegelände (Exhibition Complex)

The radio tower has been a Berlin landmark since it was ceremoniously opened in 1926 at the Third German Radio Exhibition. By present standards it is not very high at just 138 metres (150 metres with the antenna), but when it was built it was a sensation. Where the Eiffel Tower needed a ground area of 129 by 129 metres for a height of 300 metres, the radio tower had a ground area of just 20 by 20 metres. The base to height ratio for the Eiffel Tower is 1:2.3, for the radio tower it is 1:6.9 – a figure that only reinforced concrete towers can surpass.

The steel structure weighs only 400 tonnes, and at a height of 55 metres it carries a two-storey structure that overhangs by 5 metres and contains a restaurant. At a height of 125 metres is the viewing platform.

The Exhibition Complex which now encompasses the radio tower goes back to plans by Martin Wagner and Hans Poelzig from the year 1928. They envisaged a circular plan for the exhibition halls so that the visitor could go through them even in rainy weather without getting wet. An oval exhibition building was to correspond to the "Haus des Rundfunks" (House of Radio) across the road. Instead, a 35-metre-high hall of honour was built in 1934–36 to plans by Richard Ermisch, with an entrance hall flanked by two 100-metre-long hall wings. The facades reflect the vertical orientation of the Haus des Rundfunks, but they cast its expressiveness into a rigid monumentalism. Ermisch's overall plan was never implemented; a large part of the exhibition halls, as well as the older halls on the present site of the bus and coach station (from 1914 and 1924) were destroyed in the Second World War. The present Exhibition Complex contains different structures, styles and materials.

Prime examples of the airy and elegant architecture of the 1950s are two structures by Bruno Grimmek: the George C. Marshall House with the ERP Pavilion (1950 with Werner Düttmann) and the Palais

am Funkturm (1957). The Exhibition Complex was expanded to the south in 1990–99. The floor plans and the facades of the new halls were designed by Oswald Mathias Ungers as a square grid. The new, semi-circular South Entrance impresses with its clarity.

The Deutschlandhalle (Germany Hall), situated to the south-west, was built in 1935 for the Olympic games as what was then the largest multi-functional hall in the world. Since 2005 there have been plans to demolish it, although it is a historic landmark. To the east of the Exhibition Complex, connected by a bridge, is the International Congress Centre (ICC), which was built in 1975–79.

Classical Modernism / Modernism
Radio tower: Heinrich Straumer 1924–26
Charlottenburg, Masurenallee 1
Open: Radio Tower: Mon 10–20 hrs., Tues–Sat 10–23 hrs., Tel. 30 38 29 96
▷ U Kaiserdamm, S Messe-Nord / ICC

Abspannwerk Leibniz / MetaHaus
(Transformer Station Leibniz / MetaHaus)

By 1 October 1920 Berlin was the largest and third most populated city in the world (after London and New York). Berlin and seven other cities, 59 municipalities and 27 districts made up greater Berlin. One year later a plan was approved for a unified power generation and distribution system in Berlin that was in effect in East Berlin until the 1980s and in West Berlin until the 1990s. The electricity generated in the power stations located on the outskirts of Berlin was distributed – as 30 kV three-phase current – to ten transformer stations located throughout the city, where it was transformed into 6 kV and from there the electricity was distributed to smaller sub stations and bases, which, in turn, provided the city's households with 220V three-phase current. "Bewag", Berlin's electrical company, was founded to implement the plan. The management of the Bewag construction office was assumed by the architect Hans Müller (he never used his second name Heinrich), who had been the municipal director of building of Steglitz. In just six years, between 1924 and 1930, ten transformer stations and about fifty sub stations were built in and around Berlin, most of which still exist and are easily recognizable because of their distinctive architecture, although each structure was individually designed.

Brick structures, their designs are clear and sleek, with distinctive heavy cornice features and few expressionist decorative elements. The walls are often only broken up by closely situated tall and narrow windows, and the frequent use of towers and set-backs provide the structures with certain liveliness. In their proportions, the transformer stations fit in well with their surroundings, and yet, through their materials and sleek lines, they are almost archaic forms and possess an aura of distance and secrecy, which fits perfectly with their purpose. Ultimately, electricity is an invisible, deadly power that remains mysterious to laymen.

The Transformer Station Leibniz in Charlottenburg was constructed in 1925 in just seven months and was expanded to include a

railway line in 1952. The utility rooms face a long narrow interior courtyard, and the emergency staircases are located in the corners of the building and are recognizable from the outside because of their vertical window openings. The large brick walls are other-wise without structure, and two rows of small framed windows appear on the cable floor. The building is set back slightly from the Leibnizstrasse, and its distinctive cornice under the roof edge intensifies the sense of monumentality. Between 1996 and 2001 the architect couple, Petra and Paul Kahlfeldt turned the building into "MetaHaus" with office and creative space.

Other noteworthy Müller structures can be found on Zimmer-strasse (the former disco E-Werk), on Kopenhagener Strasse in Prenzlauer Berg (the former Vitra Design Museum) and on Kott-busser Ufer in Kreuzberg (event venue).

Classical Modernism
Hans (Heinrich) Müller 1925; Renovation Petra and Paul Kahlfeldt
1996–2001
Charlottenburg, Leibnizstrasse
▷ S Savignyplatz

Schaubühne am Lehniner Platz
(Theatre on Lehniner Platz)

The buildings he created in 1926–28 for "Woga" on Kurfürsten-damm are Erich Mendelsohn's largest implemented project. A complete street block on the lower part of Kurfürstendamm was to be developed with a hotel, a cinema, a cabaret theatre, residential accommodation and shops.

The brilliant feature of Mendelsohn's design is the sub-division into four different buildings. The flat cabaret complex, which now houses a pizza restaurant, a discotheque and the main building with the cinema, now the theatre "Schaubühne am Lehniner Platz", are separated by a small road (a cul-de-sac, now a pedestrian area). This public zone is completed at the rear by the six-storey former hotel building resting on pillars. Behind that on Cicero-strasse is the elongated residential building with its horizontal brick bands, its protruding balconies and the narrow, rounded entrance zones.

The structure of the present Schaubühne building can be explained by reference to the interior. As Mendelsohn wrote: "External structure developed from the layout arrangement. Two-storey line of shops around the outside, entrance and ticket hall, auditorium with slightly sloping tortoise roof becoming narrower to the rear, lift shaft for the screen, ventilation chimney with nar-row advertising tower continued forward to Kurfürstendamm."

With this ensemble, Mendelsohn breaks up the strict line of buildings aligned with the edge of the block along Kurfürsten-damm, but without leaving a hole. He visually widens the street context to create a plaza, attracts passers-by into the shopping alley by the round elements of the two end buildings, but the link to the height of the surrounding buildings is created by the former ventilation tower and the residential block.

Mendelsohn was in the process of overcoming his Expressionist phase. We still see the horizontal window bands, the stepped building structures and, not least, the wedge-like wall slab project-

ing over the end of the round building, but the complex is no longer an imposed dynamic facade like in the Mossehaus. The Ku'damm ensemble is aimed at passers-by, it portrays relaxation, and no longer an overwhelming energy and movement. This is underlined by the warm reddish brown colour of the facing bricks which form a clear contrast with the rendered facade of the former hotel.

In the conversion of the former cinema building for use as the theatre "Schaubühne" in 1976–81, the interior was completely changed.

A further remarkable building by Erich Mendelsohn is the building of the IG-Metall (metalworkers trade union) on Alte Jakobstrasse in Kreuzberg. Here, too, horizontal window bands are dominant, but the corners are no longer rounded and the whole block gives a calm impression.

Classical Modernism (New Rationalism)
Erich Mendelsohn 1926–28; alterations: Jürgen Sawade 1976–81
Wilmersdorf, Kurfürstendamm 153
www.schaubuehne.de
▷ U Adenauerplatz

Hufeisensiedlung Britz
(Britz Horseshoe Estate)

Public-assisted, low-cost housing, which is now commonplace, was an enormous challenge in the 1920s. Only large-scale residential estates seemed to offer a remedy for the chronic shortage of accommodation. For tenement dwellers to be able to afford a move, the rent cost had to be low – so the building costs had to be low, too. This was a welcome challenge for town planners and architects. Martin Wagner, the building councillor in Berlin from 1926, regarded the large residential estate in Britz as an opportunity to conduct "studies on economic building".

The concept was linked with idealistic reform enthusiasm and programmatic pathos. The estates were regarded as a departure from the oppressing tenement complexes, and their architecture was designed to reflect a sense of community among the residents. The heart of the Britz estate, the horseshoe, was a manifesto of the new type of building.

The technical implementation was not to be hidden, it was to be emphasised instead. "The individual and the whole receives its form from the meaning that it has", commented Bruno Taut in 1929.

The large-scale Britz residential estate, which was known by its central element as the "horseshoe estate", was built from 1925–33 (in seven phases of construction) to plans by Bruno Taut. The over 1000 flats are standardised with just four floor plans. All buildings are connected as rows, and each terraced house has its own tenant's garden (which originally also applied within the horseshoe). Martin Wagner designed the residential block at Stavenhagener Strasse 4–32 with the prominent staircases.

To avoid monotony, individual blocks were set forward or back, spaces widened out to plazas, buildings set in rows with symmetry and variety and especially colour – the cheapest design element – were used as instruments to give each street its own character.

The "functional" and necessarily simple architecture was often effective because of its details. Where the details are changed – with recessed windows instead of windows with glazing bars, rough plaster instead of smooth, new colours, new doors, new paving slabs etc. – this often removes the artistic value and effect. Only those with an eye for detail will discover the charm of this architecture – and discover with sorrow how often the buildings on the estate have been disfigured by small alterations.

Other estates by Bruno Taut include Falkenberg garden city (the "paintbox estate"), the extension of the "Paradies" estate, both in Treptow-Altglienicke, the "Freie Scholle" (free clod of earth) in Tegel and the large estate "Onkel-Toms-Hütte" in Zehlendorf.

Classical Modernism (New Rationalism / Expressionism)
Bruno Taut, Martin Wagner; core area 1925–27; extensions up to 1933
Neukölln (Britz)
▷ U Blaschkoallee, U Parchimer Allee

Ringsiedlung Siemensstadt (Siemensstadt Ring Estate) and Siedlung Charlottenburg-Nord

Like the horseshoe estate in Britz (cf. p. 130f.), Onkel-Toms-Hütte in Zehlendorf and the "Weisse Stadt" (white city) in Reinickendorf, the large estate in Siemensstadt was also presented at the International Building Exhibition in 1931. The aim of the construction programme was to create small flats for low-wage Siemens workers (as purely dormitory accommodation) and to try out the latest insight in urban development – the creation of long blocks. Hans Scharoun designed the urban development plan, and the individual buildings were designed by members of the architects' association "Der Ring". All buildings consisted of several storeys, and the room sizes and floor plans were standardised (with an average of 54 square metres in a two-room flat for a family of four).

From Siemensdamm in the south, two funnel-shaped building complexes by Scharoun show the way into the estate. The left-hand building, with its unusual balcony and roof forms, is often referred to by the local people as "armoured cruiser A". Scharoun himself lived there for many years.

Beyond the S-Bahn urban railway line are the long blocks by Walter Gropius along Jungfernheideweg with their wide windows and, in some cases, with roof terraces. The gatehouse on the left is part of the estate "Heimat" (1930–34 by Hans Hertlein). By comparison with the traditional appearance of this complex, the innovative elements of the "ring estate" become especially clear. To the right along Goebelstrasse are the parallel long blocks by Hugo Häring with their protruding curved balconies and striking roof zones, and at the east two long blocks by Fred Forbat. They are all oriented in a north to south direction to make the best use of light. At the southern edge of the estate is the "Langer Jammer" (Long lamentation), a curved long building with 25 identical house units (by Otto Bartning). In the north, the estate is linked to the Jungfernheide public park by the lower long blocks by Paul Rudolf Henning.

After the Second World War, Scharoun implemented his concept of an "urban landscape" in the adjacent estate to the east, Charlottenburg-Nord (between the southern edge of the park and Halemweg underground station). He overcame the monotony of long building blocks by grouping residential blocks of differing heights and types into so-called "residential clusters". The individual designs and the restriction to 310 units per cluster were aimed to give the residents a feeling of belonging. The round windows of the staircases betray the fact that Scharoun also designed the "Philharmonie". Other architects who contributed to the estate were Werner Weber and Hans Hoffmann.

Classical Modernism (New Rationalism) / Post-war period
Hans Scharoun, Walter Gropius, Otto Bartning, Hugo Häring and others
1929–31 / 1956–61
Charlottenburg
▷ U Siemensdamm, U Halemweg

Haus des Rundfunks (House of Radio)

The oldest (self-contained) radio house in the world is in Charlottenburg in Berlin.

In 1929, Hans Poelzig was successful in a competition with a design which was to be exemplary. His main idea was to place the three large broadcasting rooms in the centre of the building, shielded from street noise by the surrounding office wings. From the ends of the 150 metre long main frontage on Masurenallee, two wings recede in a convex curve and form an obtuse-angled triangle. In the middle are three trape- zoidal broadcasting rooms which are arranged around the large open courtyard behind the main front, thus forming four inner courtyards.

An impressive feature is the five-storey main frontage, in which the central 32 window axes are raised by one storey. The monumental facade is vertically structured – projection strips faced with reddish brown ceramic tiles contrast with the black brick facing of the wall surface.

Since 1987, the main hall spanning five storeys, with its galleries clad with yellow brick and its two striking lights, has again been visible in its old splendour. At the centre is the 1930 sculpture "Grosse Nacht" (Great night) by Georg Kolbe.

Hans Poelzig was not a radical reformer like Gropius, Mies van der Rohe and Le Corbusier. He refused "to experiment independently again and again without any reason", and he aimed for a freedom "which is fought for by mental processing and overcoming of the traditional, and which has nothing in common with the lack of restraint which automatically leads to bewilderment".

But he nevertheless created buildings with an expressiveness and, in many cases, a monumentalism that are still fascinating today. Poelzig frequently alternated between horizontal structures – which he used even before Mendelsohn – such as the Babylon cinema in the "Scheunenviertel" (where he was respon-

sible for the new urban development structure) and a strictly vertical structure such as the House of Radio.

His most famous work is regarded as a model of Expressionism: the alteration of the Schumann circus as the later Friedrichstadt-palast with its splendid interior architecture reminiscent of a dripstone cave (the remains were pulled down in 1985). His largest completed project was the IG Farben complex (1928–31) in Frankfurt / Main.

Between the House of Radio and Theodor-Heuss-Platz is the rbb, previously SFB television centre built in 1963–71 to plans by Robert Tepez. With its tower it not only dominates the square, but is also a landmark visible from a long distance amongst the buildings of Berlin.

Classical Modernism (Expressionism)
Hans Poelzig 1929–31
Charlottenburg, Masurenallee 8–14
▷ U Theodor-Heuss-Platz

Berolinahaus and Alexanderhaus
(Berolina and Alexander Buildings)

In 1929 a competition was declared under the city building councillor Martin Wagner for the new design of Alexanderplatz. The
competition rules prescribed a roundabout and the creation of a
"big city plaza". The idea was for the urban architecture of Berlin
to leap from its significance as a national metropolis – represented by the Wilhelm-style buildings – to a world-class international
metropolitan city.

Traffic was almost a fetish for the modern city planners of the
1920s. In the design of the big city plaza, Wagner regarded "the
passage of traffic" as being "the primary and major element, and
the formal design and functional form is only of secondary significance". A 25 year traffic forecast was the basis of the planning,
and the buildings were to be replaced after this time. The architecture was therefore not to create anything of lasting value, merely
to be economically viable. "The 'flowing traffic' on the plaza must
be balanced by 'stationary traffic' which binds the purchasing
power of the masses of people who cross the plaza (shops, restaurants, department stores, offices etc.)." The buildings were to follow
"the walking routes of the pedestrians, i.e. the purchasing power".

Wagner also had clear concepts for the architecture, and these
concepts were reflected in the result of the competition: "The
clearest of forms which develop their characteristic artistic effect
both by day and during the night hours are a fundamental condition
of the metropolitan plaza. Light flowing in by day, and light flood-
ing out by night create a completely new identity for the plaza. Colour,
form and light (advertising) are the three main building elements."

The first prize was won by the Luckhardt brothers, whose design
envisaged uniformly designed facades which were to be structured
only by horizontal window and masonry bands and to differ only
in the height and the radius of their curved corners. But they were
not awarded the commission, nor was Mies van der Rohe, whose
uncompromising proposal envisaged seven uniform rectangular

buildings without any connection between them – instead, the commission was awarded to Peter Behrens, who had been placed second in the competition.

Only the western side of the plaza was implemented in 1930 / 31. The Alexanderhaus (photo), headquarters of the Berliner Sparkasse since its renovation in 1993–95, and the Berolinahaus are eight-storey structures with one storey of shops, a protruding glass gallery for restaurants and exhibitions and six office storeys with recessed panels of two or three windows. With their glass staircases facing each other, they create a visual gateway towards Rathausstrasse and the S-Bahn urban railway station. The bottom floors of the Berolinahaus were gutted during restoration work in 2005 / 06. In 2006 the clothing chain C&A opened its largest store in Germany; the Dutch company opened its first German store in 1911 on Alexanderplatz.

Classical Modernism (New Rationalism)
Peter Behrens 1930 / 31
Mitte, Alexanderplatz 1 / 2
▷ S / U Alexanderplatz

Shell-Haus (Shell Building)

This office building is an essential entry in any architectural guide to classical modernism – and for many it is the most striking facade of the 1920s. Emil Fahrenkamp's Shell building by the Landwehrkanal was built in 1930–32 as the main headquarters of the Shell subsidiary Rhenania-Ossag mineral oil company. It was subsequently also used by the neighbouring naval high command, and after the war it became the main headquarters of the Berlin electricity board, Bewag. Since its renovation in 2000 the building has been used by the Gasag gas company.

The characteristic feature of the building is the main facade which leaps forward in six stages, while at the same time increasing in height from six storeys (five at the rear) to ten storeys. The edges of the building are rounded, and even the windows around the corners describe a quarter-circle. The walls between the horizontal window bands are clad with Roman travertine.

The facade has no vertical sub-division at all; the gentle wave-like structure, the step-by-step upward flow to the rectangular tower block and the emphasis on the horizontal create an effective background, especially when seen from Potsdamer Strasse.

The building consists of four wings grouped around a four-sided inner courtyard. The tall west wing, the rear north wing and the receding east wing are at right angles to each other. In the oblique south wing, the steps in the facade are absorbed by the floor layout of the front office rooms, whereas the inside corridor and the rear offices overlooking the courtyard are rectangular.

Just a few bus stops away is a further milestone in Berlin's office block architecture: the Kathreiner building next to Kleistpark on Potsdamer Strasse. In 1929 / 30 Bruno Paul built the first inner-city tower building in Berlin with twelve storeys and two lower side wings. Here, too, the travertine-clad facade is purely horizontal in structure, but the corners of the building are emphatically an-

gular. The vertical band of windows on the end of the tower block acts as a vertical counterweight.

A third example of a horizontal facade design, again with rounded projecting elements, is the Tauentzien palace in Nürnberger Strasse (1928–31 by Bielenberg and Moser, today Hotel Ellington).

Although all three buildings are dynamic and "expressive" in their appearance, they are regarded as belonging to the "New Rationalism" style because of their smooth facades, their horizontal structure and their lack of ornamentation.

Classical Modernism (New Rationalism)
Emil Fahrenkamp 1930–32
Tiergarten, Reichpietschufer 60 / corner of Stauffenbergstrasse
▷ Bus M29, 148

Auswärtiges Amt (Foreign Office)

The former Reichsbank, now the Foreign Office, was the first large new building of the National Socialist regime in Berlin. In February 1933 a long-prepared competition was declared in which, according to a commemorative publication of 1934, "30 of the best-known architects from all German districts" participated including Gropius, Poelzig and Mies van der Rohe, whose design was shortlisted. But Hitler then decided personally in favour of the plan of the Reichsbank building director Heinrich Wolff, which had existed previously. Before the end of 1933, work began to demolish several streets with historical buildings from the 18th and 19th century, including the old "Münze" by Stüler. The new building was dedicated in 1940.

On the irregular curved ground layout, a four wing complex was built with its inner longitudinal axis occupied by a court of honour and three cashier halls. The five to seven storey steel frame building is clad with light-coloured sandstone, the facades are without any structural elements apart from the ground floor, which is emphasised by columns in front of the recessed wall.

The Reichsbank competition is interesting in that it reflects the state of architectural discussion at the end of the Weimar Republic. The 30 participants had been selected before the National Socialists seized power, but they were mainly architects of the conservative and traditionalist direction. Functionalist modernism made outstanding achievements in the 1920s, but it was often not appreciated by the public at large. Especially after the economic crisis of 1929, conservative architects and developers dominated the scene. The year 1933 was therefore not a radical change in the development of German architecture. Although the modernists were soon ridiculed and in some cases driven into exile, there was no fundamentally new departure in architecture, not even a specific architectural language. The most important construction tasks related to the state and party buildings which expressed a rigid

and monumental neo-classicism. In industrial buildings, however, which were purely functional buildings without any ideological overtones, New Rationalism lived on, whereas in the construction of residential estates, which never reached the level of the 1920s in spite of the shortage of accommodation, a nostalgic conventional style was prevalent.

After the war, the Reichsbank building became the headquarters of the GDR Ministry of Finance, and from 1959 it was the party headquarters of the ruling SED communist party (and the seat of the Politburo). Since the relocation of the German government in 1999 it has been used by the Foreign Office. The extension work was planned by the architects Thomas Müller and Ivan Reimann.

Anti-modernism (National Socialist Traditionalism)
Heinrich Wolff 1933–40; extension work: Thomas Müller, Ivan Reimann 1997–99
Mitte, Werderscher Markt
www.auswaertiges-amt.de
▷ U Hausvogteiplatz, bus 100, 147

Detlev-Rohwedder-Haus
(Detlev Rohwedder Building)

The former Reich Air Travel Ministry is the most striking relic of the former government district on Wilhelmstrasse, and with over 2000 rooms it is the largest office building in Europe. After the war it was used by various GDR authorities as a ministry building. From 1990 it was occupied for several years by the "Treuhand-Anstalt" (government privatisation agency), and it now bears the name of the assassinated former director of the agency. In 1999 the Federal Ministry of Finance moved in.

The government district had developed after 1871 when Bismarck chose Palais Schulenburg on Wilhelmplatz (at the junction of Mohrenstrasse, now built over) as the official residence of the Reich Chancellor, and in the ensuing period numerous Prussian and Reich ministries moved into the vicinity. The Reich Chancellery, which was given a monumental new wing along Vossstrasse in 1938 / 39, was destroyed, but one wing of the Ministry of Propaganda from 1934–40 survived on Mauerstrasse.

In 1935 / 36 the Reich Air Travel Ministry followed with a group of buildings which integrated the complex of the former Prussian Herrenhaus (on Leipziger Strasse, current seat of the Federal Council) and the Prussian parliament (Niederkirchnerstrasse, now the seat of the Berlin federal state parliament). At the end of the 1930s there were discussions on the possibility of erecting another building corresponding to the Air Travel Ministry on the other side of Wilhelmstrasse (as the Reich Post Office Ministry), but because of the war these plans did not get past the preliminary stage.

Clearance work for Göring's new ministry building on Wilhelmstrasse began at the beginning of 1935, and 1000 rooms were ready for occupation as early as October of the same year. The entire complex was completed in 1936. Construction work went on around the clock, and many parts were prefabricated. The speed of the demolition and construction work represented a deliberate

policy to demonstrate the energy and determination of the new regime – in fact, state propaganda frequently portrayed Berlin as an enormous building site.

The four to seven storey office complex was built around three inner courtyards and four courts which open out to an older park at the rear. The main entrance is situated in a court of honour on Wilhelmstrasse and is at the same time the axis of symmetry.

The reinforced concrete framework is filled with pumice concrete cavity blocks and clad with silver grey shell limestone panels. The ground layout and structure are functional, but the facade cladding transforms it from a framework structure to a solid stone building. Contemporary architecture critics acclaimed it as a "majestic building" which "shows an attitude which preserves Prussian distinctiveness in its fundamental elements".

Anti-modernism (National Socialist Traditionalism)
Ernst Sagebiel 1935 / 36
Mitte, Leipziger Strasse 5–7 / corner of Wilhelmstrasse
www.bundesfinanzministerium.de
▷ U Stadtmitte, U Kochstrasse

Olympiastadion (Olympic Stadium)

Three times Berlin applied to be the site of the Olympic Games: in 1916, 1936 and 2000. All three projects envisaged the Olympic Stadium in Charlottenburg as the main venue – a work of the architectural family March.

In 1909, Otto March built a 2400 metre long horse-racing track in the northernmost section of the Grunewald forest. When the 1916 Olympic Games were awarded to Berlin, the German stadium was built within this racing track in 1912 / 13. To ensure that the racing track could still be used, March built the oval stadium in a hollow in the ground as an "earth stadium".

The largest sports stadium in the world at the time (40 000 spectators) was a modern reinforced concrete structure with bombastic historical architecture; it was especially used for ceremonial and military purposes. The "College of physical exercise", which was founded in 1922, then formed the core of the "German sports forum" which Otto March's sons Werner and Walter built as the winners of a competition in 1925–28.

In 1931, when Berlin was awarded the 1936 Olympic Games, Werner March was given the task of redesigning the German stadium. But the National Socialists recognised the immense prestige potential of the Games and had a new "Reich sports field" built, for which Werner March was able to draw on old concepts.

The strictly symmetrical complex was then built up to 1936 with the Olympischer Platz, the Olympic Stadium lowered to 12 metres below ground level and with space for 110 000 spectators, the "Maifeld", a marching ground for 500 000 people with a grandstand overshadowed by the Langemarck hall of the Olympic tower which rises to a height of 78 metres, and finally the present "Waldbühne" outdoor theatre for 25 000 spectators. Other facilities were a hockey stadium, a riding stadium, a swimming stadium and the extensive complex of the German sports forum; the smooth integration of these facilities into the overall complex shows the con-

tinuity of the monumental architectural style from the 1920s into the National Socialist period.

After the war, part of the complex was accessible for public use and part was used by the British occupation forces. The restoration of the "Glockenturm" (bell tower) from 1960–62 was again directed by Werner March.

Between 2000 and 2004 the Olympic Stadium was renovated and modernized by the Hamburg architectural firm, gmp · Gerkan, Marg & Partner. A new roof, which had continuous flood lighting and provided protection for all 75 000 seats, was added. The field was lowered several levels and was given a blue tartan track, the colour of the city's football club, Hertha BSC. The final game of the 2006 World Cup was played here.

Anti-modernism (National Socialist Traditionalism)
Werner March 1934–36
Charlottenburg, Olympischer Platz 3
Open: 9 hrs. to dusk, Tel. 25 00 23 22
www.olympiastadion-berlin.de
▷ U Olympia-Stadion, S Olympiastadion

Flughafen Tempelhof (Tempelhof Airport)

Like many buildings from the National Socialist period, Tempelhof Airport is impressive because of its sheer size and monumentalism. The architect Ernst Sagebiel was listed twice in the Guinness Book of Records – once for the largest office building in Europe (the former Air Travel Ministry) and once for the largest building of the continent, Tempelhof airport, built from 1936–1941 and designed to be the largest air travel junction in Europe. It replaced a complex that was only a few years old with an airfield that was opened in 1923.

Access to the complex is via Platz der Luftbrücke. The quarter-circle office development (once the main headquarters of Lufthansa) forms a large central court in front of the reception building. The 100-metre-long departure hall is the symmetrical axis of the total complex and leads to the flight gate hall, which is 400 metres long and has a roof without any central supports. The hangars directly join both sides of this hall, forming a curved building with a total length of 1200 metres. The long front is structured and monumentalised by block-type staircase towers at intervals of 70 metres. The entire roof is designed as a viewing terrace from which spectators can watch flight demonstrations.

The facade design is typical of its period. The reinforced concrete framework is clad with shell limestone panels. The endless rows of windows are simply "cut into" the wall, only the facade of the reception building is more intricate in its design.

The airport was closed for public flights in 1975, then reopened in 1985 and shut permanently on 30 October 2008. The landmark structure is now a venue for fairs and for cultural and sporting events; various possible long-term uses for the complex are being debated. The 220-hectare open space has been accessible to the public since May 2010. A long-term use being discussed is for smaller areas of the grounds to have houses built it, while the majority of the space would be used as a park. The 2017 International Garden Show is supposed to take place here.

On Platz der Luftbrücke the Airlift Memorial, known as the "hunger rake", commemorates the supply of West Berlin from the air during the Soviet blockade in 1948 / 49.

In 1975 Tempelhof was replaced by Tegel Airport, which is further away from the city and was trendsetting in its design as a "drive-in airport". The basic idea is that passengers can arrive by car or bus directly in front of the respective flight gates. The flight gates are arranged round the outside of a hexagon, and access is via an inner circular road. The tower is situated separately, and the original plan was for a further hexagon to be built to the east of the tower to double the total capacity. The architects were Meinhard von Gerkan, who is also building the new Lehrter central station, Volkwin Marg and Klaus Nickels.

Anti-modernism (National Socialist Traditionalism)
Ernst Sagebiel 1936–41
Tempelhof, Platz der Luftbrücke
▷ U Platz der Luftbrücke

Russische Botschaft (Russian Embassy)

Only one building violates the so-called "Linden statute" imposed by royal order in that it has a court of honour and exceeds the prescribed eaves height. It is no accident that this building is the Russian Embassy which was built in 1950–53 as the embassy of the USSR in Berlin, the capital of the GDR (which was the official term for East Berlin). The imposing complex was built on the site of the old embassy, which was destroyed in the war and was an 18th century rococo palace which had been classically altered in 1837 by Eduard Knoblauch, the architect of the new synagogue. The new complex also integrated further plots on Behrenstrasse and Glinkastrasse to create a small diplomatic estate which even had its own swimming pool.

The new embassy built under the direction of Friedrich Skujin set the trend for the appearance of GDR architecture in subsequent years: a mixture of Stalinist neo-classicism and national building traditions, which in Germany meant falling back on Schinkel.

On the side facing Unter den Linden, the four-storey building extends around a large court of honour. In its basic arrangement it is reminiscent of the original ground layout of the Prince Heinrich Palace, the present Humboldt University. The tall, protruding central section is crowned by a cubic lantern which is similar in appearance to the blunt towers of the Pergamon museum. Below it is the large dome room which leads on via the elaborate main staircase to the festival room in the centre of the block. The side wings around the court of honour contain smaller halls and splendid rooms, and the end buildings facing the street contain ministerial apartments. The office accommodation is in the rear by Behrenstrasse.

The individual elements of the ashlar stone clad facade are derived from the classical repertoire which was also used by Berlin classicism of the early 19th century: colossal pilasters, a rusticated pedestal, band-type corners, a roof ledge with attic and

the form of the window parapets. But the effect is completely different – the architectural language is clearly Stalinist, which is expressed in the cold monumentalism and the uncompromising austerity.

The embassies of Hungary, replaced today by a new building, and Poland on the opposite side of the street were completely unpretentious behind functionalist facades, whereas the embassy of the Czechoslovakia, now used by the Czech Republic, occupied a monumental building on Wilhelmstrasse in the typical 1970s / 1980s style.

Anti-modernism (Stalinist Neo-classicism)
Collectives of Stryshewski / Lebedinskij / Sichert / Skujin 1950–53
Mitte, Unter den Linden 63–65
▷ S / U Brandenburger Tor, bus 100

Karl-Marx-Allee

After devastating war damage, the buildings constructed in 1952–60 along the almost two kilometres between Strausberger Platz and Frankfurter Tor were probably the most monumental 20th century street development in Germany. The road was widened to 90 metres, the seven to nine storey buildings were built in accordance with party instructions (and contrary to the designs in an urban development competition) in the Stalinist / neo-classical style of the 1950s (photo). Shops and restaurants were situated in the lower one or two storeys, and the upper storeys contained apartments which were comfortable by the standards of the time. The building blocks are up to 300 metres long and vary by protruding and receding sections and different numbers of storeys; the facades are decorated in some places with ornamental ceramic tiles. Following Moscow's instructions, national elements were integrated – in Berlin this meant details based on forms of the Schinkel period. The individual sections of the development were built under the direction of various collectives.

By contrast, the balcony access gallery buildings at Karl-Marx-Allee 102 / 104 and 126 / 128, which are based on designs by the first city building councillor installed by the Soviets, Hans Scharoun, and were erected before the beginning of the "national reconstruction programme", are completely dominated by the functionalist style of the 1920s.

The first building in the new style, which was programmatic for the further development, was the nine storey "tall building" at Weberwiese which was built in 1951 / 52 by the collective Hermann Henselmann. The two towers by Frankfurter Tor became the symbolic landmark of the street. They roughly correspond to the forms of the Gontard towers on Gendarmenmarkt, and like the buildings around Strausberger Platz they were designed by Henselmann.

As the "first Socialist street" on German soil, the Stalinallee, as

it was called until 1961, for many years drew violent criticism and opposition from the west.

However, even with its questionable neo-classicism and monumentalism, the development of this main street respected the historically developed urban setting. This aspect was given up later under the pressure of economic considerations – and western examples. The clearest example is the continuation of rebuilding between Strausberger Platz and Alexanderplatz. Moreover, the limited funds also led to a radical change in the building techniques and formal language.

Noteworthy buildings on Karl-Marx-Allee also include the two functionalist cinemas "Kosmos" and "International" (1960–62).

Anti-modernism (Stalinist Neo-classicism)
Collectives of Hartmann, Henselmann, Hopp, Leucht, Paulick, Souradny
1952–60
Friedrichshain, Karl-Marx-Allee
▷ U Strausberger Platz, U Weberwiese, U Frankfurter Tor

Allianz-Versicherung
(Allianz Insurance Building)

Our image of (western) architecture of the 1950s is characterised by sweeping generalisations and prejudices, even though we are now beginning to see this era in a more differentiated manner. From the end of the war until the 1970s, new residential accommodation was especially needed. Architecture was characterised by residential and estate buildings, and the results were often no more than mediocre – and in some cases a failure when seen with hindsight. The suggestions from the 1920s such as Taut's concept of the residential estate degenerated to mere schematic building; variety gave way to repetition; in face of the enormous building task, architecture lost sight of the details and nuances which are necessary to avoid falling into boredom and monotony in rational, simplified post-Bauhaus buildings.

Examples of this tendency can be found in abundance in all West German cities, including Berlin. But there were and are a number of outstanding buildings, although many of them have now been deformed by slight alterations.

Perhaps one of the most beautiful buildings of the 1950s, and a model for subsequent office buildings, was the Berlin headquarters of the Allianz insurance company on Joachimstaler Platz. The complex consists of a 14 storey tower block, the first to be built on Kurfürstendamm, an elongated six storey wing which is also slightly curved and which widens Joachimstaler Strasse into a plaza, and an end building facing Kurfürstendamm. The travertine-clad reinforced concrete structure of the tower block, with the vertical band-type structure of the facade which creates a monumental lightness, dominates the urban setting. The shop zone on the ground floor is separated from the office storeys by an overhanging roof.

Another tower block with a similar structure is the Hamburg-Mannheimer insurance building at Kurfürstendamm 32, which was built in 1955–56 by Hans Gerber and Otto Risse. The office build-

ing of the Chamber of Commerce and Industry (IHK) in Hardenberg-strasse (1954 / 55 by Franz Heinrich Sobotka and Gustav Müller) also follows the architectural language of the 1920s with its vertical structure and the roof projecting over the high ground floor – thus forming a welcome contrast to contemporary functional buildings such as the adjacent extension of the Federal Administrative Court.

In front of the Allianz building is a redundant relic of the 1950s, the traffic control stand which was once built for the traffic lights on the corner. Across the street is a further notable ensemble from the 1950s: Café Kranzler and the former Bilka department store (now Karstadt Sport), both built in 1956–58 by Hans Dustmann.

Post-war Modernism West (Expressionist Reminiscence)
Alfred Gunzenhauser, Paul Schwebes 1953–55
Joachimstaler Strasse 10–12 / corner of Kurfürstendamm
▷ U Kurfürstendamm

Hansaviertel (Hansa District)

A description of the Hansaviertel would fill a whole book. 36 individual buildings or ensembles still form the prime specimen of modern architecture and urban planning of the 1950s. The southern section of the war-ravaged Hansa district between the S-Bahn urban railway line and Tiergarten was selected as the central demonstration area of the International Building Exhibition to present the "city of tomorrow" – in a deliberate contrast to Stalinallee and the restored tenement districts in East-Berlin. The result of the urban planning competition carried out in 1953 envisaged loose structures and a gradual transition to the Tiergarten instead of the closed block structure of the pre-war era. 53 architects from all parts of the world were invited to design 45 structures, of which 35 were finally implemented. The final development plan was settled under the direction of Otto Bartning. The participating architects were all adherents of the "modernist" movement committed to "new building", including Aalvar Aalto, Egon Eiermann, Walter Gropius, Arne Jacobsen, Wassili Luckhardt, Oscar Niemeyer, Sep Ruf, Paul Schneider-Esleben, Hans Schwippert and Max Taut. The photograph shows the ten-storey tall narrow apartment house by Walter Gropius and Wils Ebert.

The buildings are mostly "solitary" blocks unconnected to the adjacent buildings and therefore without any clear front and rear. Around the central complex on Hansaplatz with the single storey shop passage, the church, cinema (now the Grips theatre), library and kindergarten arose a loose mixture of high and low buildings surrounded by much greenery with long blocks of various height and isolated 16 and 17 storey tower blocks in the subsidised public housing scheme and two-storey single family and multiple family houses for independently funded house owners – plus a second church and the exhibition building of the "Berlin-Pavillon" next to Tiergarten S-Bahn station. On a plot of land where a number of single family houses were planned but

not built, the Academy of the Arts was built in 1959–60 by Werner Düttmann.

The architecture of the 1950s can be regarded as an aesthetic counter-movement to Speer's neo-classicism and an ethical breach with the recent past. Not reconstruction but a radical new beginning was demanded, "a-historical simplicity", "from the spirit of the victims" as it was worded 1947 in a declaration by famous architects including Max Taut, Schwippert and Eiermann. And that meant – following on from the Bauhaus movement – reinforced concrete buildings, clarity of structure and open floor plans. After the war years in bomb shelters, a liberating brightness was now the aim in residential premises.

Post-war Modernism West
1953–57, various architects
Tiergarten
▷ U Hansaplatz, S Tiergarten, S Bellevue

Haus der Kulturen der Welt
(House of the Cultures of the World)

The Congress Hall was the US American contribution to the International Building Exhibition in 1957. It was declared as a gift of America to its close affiliate of West Berlin.

On the basis of plans by Hugh A. Stubbins and with the cooperation of Werner Düttmann and Franz Mocken, a technically revolutionary building was built on the south bank of the Spree in the middle of the Tiergarten, and it was regarded as a great artistic achievement and has frequently been copied. The people of Berlin soon gave the building a fitting nickname: the "pregnant oyster".

Above a base storey measuring 92 by 96 metres rises the wide sweep of the roof structure. The roof is supported on both sides by steel anchors which only rest on two points. The base storey is generously glazed on both sides and comprises three staggered levels with the large reception hall, a cafeteria, a theatre auditorium with 400 seats, an exhibition area, further smaller rooms for congresses, seminars and the administration and, on the side facing the Spree, a two-storey restaurant.

The hall itself contains the auditorium. Because of the almost round floor plan, the stage at one side is comparatively wide and shallow, and the rising rows of seats for the audience become increasingly wide. The auditorium seats 1250.

In the central axis of the entrance side – facing away from the river – a large outdoor flight of steps leads to the terrace which is rarely used because the entrance is in the base storey. In front of the building is an impressive large pond, in the middle of which Henry Moore's bronze sculpture "Big butterfly" can be seen.

In 1980 part of the roof collapsed because the steel core of the front roof arch had rusted through. Although there was no concept for its use, the hall was reconstructed for the 750 year celebrations in 1987. Since 1989 it has been used under the rather ungainly name "House of the Cultures of the World" as a site for

events and exhibitions and also for Berlin festivals such as the jazz festival in November and, for a time, the Berlinale (film festival) in February.

Near the vehicle entrance, a 40 metre high bell tower was built in 1986 / 87 which contains a glockenspiel of 68 bells, the so-called carillon. The four-part pylon designed by the architects Bangert, Jansen, Scholz and Schultes is made of polished black Labrador stone.

Post-war Modernism West
Hugh A. Stubbins, Werner Düttmann, Franz Mocken 1956 / 57
Tiergarten, John-Foster-Dulles-Allee 10
Open: daily 10–19 hrs., Tel. 39 78 70
www.hkw.de
▷ Bus 100

Le-Corbusier-Haus (Le Corbusier Building)

The Le Corbusier building was also one of the demonstration projects for the building exhibition of 1957. But by contrast with the Congress Hall, Berlin's largest residential building with 1400 inhabitants is not a unique structure, it is only one of five "residential factories" designed by the Swiss architect Charles Eduoard Jeanneret, who called himself Le Corbusier.

Le Corbusier was one of the great innovators of modern architecture, radical and uncompromising. Like many of his artistic contemporaries he was fascinated by machines. He wanted to transfer the "relentlessness of mechanics" to architecture; he wanted the apartment, and even the whole city community, to work like a machine.

In the 1930s, for example, he designed reconstruction plans for Paris in which everything to the east of the Seine island would be pulled down and replaced by eighteen four-winged skyscrapers in a green park landscape.

As early as 1914 he developed his principle of a stackable house for mass residential accommodation. "A framework, completely independent of the task of the building floor plan: this framework (or skeleton) carries the floor slabs and the stairs. It is made of standard elements which can be combined with each other, which makes a great variety possible in the grouping of these buildings."

The first of his five "unités d'habitation" (residential units) was built in 1947–52. Four others followed – the third building was built in Berlin for the "Interbau". But as its dimensions were too large for the Hansaviertel, a construction site south of the Olympic Stadium was chosen. The 17 storey reinforced concrete building which rests on 7 metre high pillars contains 557 apartments: 212 small apartments with just one living room, 253 apartments with two rooms (living room / bedroom) situated one above the other and 88 three room apartments which are also distributed over two

storeys. Nine "streets" (corridors) are sufficient to provide access to all apartments.

The "urban infrastructure" of shops, kindergarten, sports hall and theatre was not implemented. In addition, the dimensions of the building in Berlin had to be altered because the authorities did not give building permission for the originally planned small interior dimensions (the basic unit "Modulator" developed for the ideal athletic human being).

"As far as I know", wrote Le Corbusier, "this is the first example in history in which it is not a ruler's palace, temple, town hall or other majestic building, but a simple house for the human being, his house, my house, the house of our fellow humans, which rises up to a monumental size without taking from any of its parts their respect for the individual, physical and subjective dimension."

Post-war Modernism West
Le Corbusier 1956–58
Charlottenburg, Flatowallee 16
▷ S Olympiastadion, bus X49, 149

Alexanderplatz

Alexanderplatz, which has been so called since the visit by Czar Alexander I. in 1805, kept its suburban character up to the middle of the 19th century. It was here that cattle markets were held, and the nearby barracks used the area as an exercise ground.

It was only after the construction of the S-Bahn urban railway network in 1882, the central market hall in 1886, the Tietz department store in 1904–11 and the underground railway from 1913 that the "Alex" developed to become the most important traffic and shopping centre for the eastern areas of Berlin. Its major landmark was the bronze "Berolina".

Due to the extension of the underground network and the daily traffic chaos, a redesign of Alexanderplatz was proposed in 1928. A roundabout was built at the centre, but the new building development to plans by Peter Behrens was only implemented in the western half (cf. p. 136f.).

After devastating damage during the war, Alexanderplatz was completely redesigned in 1966–73 and made four times larger. The core area became a pedestrian zone, and traffic was routed around the plaza on four-lane roads. The surrounding buildings arose in several phases until 1973: The "teachers' building" with the pictorial frieze by Walter Womacka and the dome of the congress hall (Hermann Henselmann 1961–64), the "Centrum" department store which is now "Kaufhof" (Josef Kaiser), the dominating 123-metre-high-hotel "Stadt Berlin", now the "Park Inn" (Roland Korn), the 17 storey "travel building" (Roland Korn), the monumental facade of the electrical industry building (Heinz Mehlan, altered in the nineties and its facade adorned with quotes from Döblin's novel "Berlin Alexanderplatz") and the publishing house Berliner Verlag (Karl-Ernst Swora). The world clock was erected in 1969.

Following German reunification, a competition took place for a new design for the area. The winning design went to Hans Kollhoff, who proposed the demolition of most of the existing structures

and the construction of thirteen high rises, a plan that remains un-
executed. With a new outdoor surface and furnishings, as well as
the return of tram stops and two new buildings, what is without a
doubt the most monumental urban square in Germany once again
has a significantly more intimate feeling: The former Centrum
department store was vastly enlarged along the square and was
given a new facade (Jan Kleihues 2004–06); the eastern side of
the Alex is now defined by the department store »die mitte«
(2007–09). Located on the other side of the Grunerstrasse, Alexa
opened in 2007 and Berlin's second largest shopping centre (after
the Gropius Passage in Wilmersdorf) has proved to be a crowd
puller. The red-coloured concrete structure has few windows and
its sparse interior decor is reminiscent of the Art Deco style.

Post-war Modernism East
Various collectives 1961–73
Mitte, Alexanderplatz
www.alexanderplatz.com
▷ S / U Alexanderplatz

Kaiser-Wilhelm-Gedächtniskirche (Emperor Wilhelm Memorial Church)

The "hollow tooth" was the symbol of the way West Berlin rose up from ruins after the war, but before its destruction the church was the symbol and landmark of the sophisticated and pleasure-seeking "new west". The "Gedächtniskirche" (the abbreviated name by which it is generally known) was built in 1891–95 to commemorate the first German emperor, Wilhelm I. on the initiative of his grandson Wilhelm II.

It was not only the outstanding urban situation at the crossing point of several major roads that attracted many donations and made the building the most impressive church in Berlin – it also benefited from the general popularity of the first German emperor and the wealth of the citizens in its parish. Franz Schwechten, the royal building councillor and the architect of such buildings as Anhalter station, designed a cross-shaped building with several spires in the style of late Rhineland Romanticism. The spire over the main facade was 113 metres high and the tallest spire in the city, and the church was correspondingly rich in its interior fittings.

After it was destroyed in the war, the initial proposal was for a glass church to be built inside the ruin, but this plan was soon dropped. A competition was declared instead, and Egon Eiermann was the prizewinner with his design for a completely new building. But the "hollow tooth" had already become a symbol, and the plans set off the greatest and most passionate architectural debate in Berlin's post-war history. Even Walter Gropius became involved and spoke of "Germany's most beautiful ruin". Eiermann was eventually persuaded into a compromise, even though he was not really convinced. The 68 metre high ruined tower was preserved (and used as an exhibition room), and it was surrounded by a four-part new building ensemble. In front of the old main portal Eiermann placed the church building, and on the site of the former nave he placed the bell tower. The entire complex is situated on a raised platform.

The spire ruin gave the inspiration for the octagonal design of the new church building, which has a simple form as a steel structure with a flat roof. The unique effect of the interior is due to the walls made up of over 22 000 blue glass window panes which are set into square concrete frames. It is only on closer inspection that the visitor realises that the church has two outer walls – partly to keep out traffic noise and partly to enhance the effect of the glass panels by using artificial light between the walls. For many architecture critics, Eiermann's new church building ranks alongside Le Corbusier's chapel in Ronchamp as the major church building of the post-war era.

Historicism / Post-war Modernism West
Franz Schwechten 1891–95; Egon Eiermann 1959–63
Breitscheidplatz
Open: church: daily 9–19 hrs., memorial hall in the spire ruin:
Mon–Sat 10–18 hrs., Sun 12–17.30 hrs., Tel. 218 50 23
www.gedaechtniskirche-berlin.de
▷ S / U Zoologischer Garten, U Kurfürstendamm, bus 100, M19, M29

Europacenter (Europe Centre)

The Europacenter was built in 1963–65 and became a symbol of West Berlin like the Gedächtniskirche; because of the revolving Mercedes star on the roof it is also known as the "i-Punkt" (the dot on the i). The 22-storey tower block is the dominant urban design element in the West Berlin city centre that developed in the 1950s and Berlin's most important contribution to the "international style", the world-wide box-type architecture which is usually based on a misunderstood imitation of the work of Mies van der Rohe.

Breitscheidplatz is the central plaza of the former West Berlin and the counterpart to Alexanderplatz in the east of the city. But whereas Alexanderplatz is coherent in its design and monumental in its effect, the architecture of Breitscheidplatz remained random and almost provisional. Even Ernst Reuter Platz, the urban setting in the west that is most similar to Alexanderplatz, is an accidental collection of individual buildings, some of them of a high standard, but without any coherent character.

The Europacenter was built on the site of the legendary "Romanisches Café" (the meeting place of literary figures in the 1920s) and is a complex of different building structures on a large area. The two storey pedestal building, which is used for shops and restaurants along with the basement, covers the entire ground area. The inner courtyards were covered in the 1970s. Other parts of the complex are the cinema on Tauentzienstrasse, Hotel Palace on Budapester Strasse, the adjacent apartment building and the 86 metre high tower block. On the side facing Breitscheidplatz, the low structure is raised by two top storeys, thus equalling the eaves height of the older buildings to the north and south of the plaza. To the north the so-called "Zentrum am Zoo" dating from the 1950s consists of several individual buildings which shield the zoo from the city. The 16 storey slab-like tower block with a facade which was clad with white panels in 1986 faces towards Hardenbergplatz. The box-shaped and completely unadorned cinema

"Zoo-Palast" is the main scene of the film festival held in February of every year (Berlinale). Along the northern edge of Breitscheidplatz is a long low building, which originally consisted of the two storey base structure with colonnades and a three storey top section resting on pillars. In 1978 the present third storey was inserted. Especially this part of the building, with its functionalist glass facade, clearly shows the influence of the architecture of the 1920s.

Post-war Modernism West (International Style)
Helmut Hentrich, Hubert Petschnigg 1963–65
New facade modelled after the original 2000 / 01
Charlottenburg, Breitscheidplatz
www.europa-center-berlin.de
▷ S / U Zoologischer Garten, U Kurfürstendamm, bus 100, M19, M29

Philharmonie

Hans Scharoun's Philharmonie was the first building in the "Kultur-forum". There had previously been a competition design for the land of the present "Freie Volksbühne" theatre near Bundesallee. But when the possibility of moving it to the southern edge of Tier-garten was considered, Scharoun sketched the plan for a cultural forum which would eliminate the old street pattern. A number of the buildings in the "privy councillor district" had already been pulled down from 1938 to make space for the "round plaza" of Speer's planned Germania. In the war the entire district was de-stroyed – only the church building of the Matthäuskirche survived.

The Philharmonie is regarded as Scharoun's major work and as a model of "organic building", a concept in which each building develops "organically" outwards from its interior use without any formal restrictions. This approach, which is geared specifically to the respective building task, brought Scharoun and the Philhar-monie much criticism from architectural critics. By contrast with buildings such as those by Mies van der Rohe, the Philharmonie was not suitable as a model for an architectural school, it was a "unique project not capable of typification" and thus did not set any trends for the further reconstruction of West Germany.

Scharoun's concern was "to give an appropriate form to a place for making music and the joint experience of music". The tradi-tional form of stage and auditorium was out of the question. Instead, Scharoun moved the orchestra into the middle of the room design which is made up of pentagons set at an angle to each other (which explains the emblem of the Philharmonie). From the lowest point of the hall, the orchestra platform, the rows of seats are combined into manageable blocks and rise in terraces ("like a vineyard") to a position almost under the roof which hangs like a tent and also determines the exterior structure. Below the auditorium is the foyer, and many a music-lover has lost his way in its bizarre labyrinth of stairs and corridors. With the dynamism

and complexity of the Philharmonie, Scharoun created a distinct contrast to the dominant buildings of the period with simple grid patterns and short distances.

From the outside, the Philharmonie appears like the bow of a ship, a motif which Scharoun often used. The facade of yellow anodised aluminium panels was only added in 1978–81, previously the building was painted in an ochre brown colour.

In 1978–84, the Musikinstrumentenmuseum (Musical Instrument Museum) was built to the north-east of the Philharmonie by Edgar Wisniewski on the basis of plans by Scharoun, who died in 1972. From 1984 to 1988 the Kammermusiksaal (Chamber Music Hall) was built on the basis of concept sketches by Scharoun and exact plans by Wisniewski.

Post-war Modernism West
Hans Scharoun 1960–63
Tiergarten, Kulturforum, Herbert-von-Karajan-Strasse 1
Tel. 25 48 80
www.berliner-philharmoniker.de
▷ S / U Potsdamer Platz, bus M29, M41, 148, 200

Neue Nationalgalerie (New National Gallery)

For the planning of the Neue Nationalgalerie, a man was commissioned whose architecture could not form a greater contrast to the architecture of Scharoun's Philharmonie. Whereas Scharoun designed his buildings in terms of their function, i.e. from the inside out, Mies van der Rohe designed buildings in which the function was subjected to the form. He said that the usage may change, but "our buildings will last for a few hundred years". With his maxim "Less is more", the architect from the Rhine paved the way for a whole generation of architects, but he was often misunderstood. For him, simplicity of form was not a means of rational, low cost building – Mies van der Rohe's buildings were often unusually expensive – but islands of structure and clarity in a chaotic environment dominated by the accumulated traditions of many centuries. His buildings are solitary designs which do not make any allowances for the surrounds, and they are neutral in their usage. The simplified steel frame structures with large glass frontages and flexible floor plans result from this principle.

But that does not mean that Mies van der Rohe was a slave to construction engineering. On the contrary: "Building means designing structures. Designing structures means thinking through every detail down to its smallest part and fashioning the whole out of the creative interplay of the details."

Thus, the effect of the Neue Nationalgalerie is not only seen in its overall structure, it can also be seen in the details. The roof is not just a simple steel panel of a certain size – in the interplay of its areas, reinforcements, edges and rivets it is the result of an artistic intention to which engineering considerations were adapted, and the same applies to the design of the glass facade and the eight steel supports. The metal roof panel with its length of 65 metres, for example, is curved upwards 10 centimetres at the centre to avoid the visual impression of a sagging roof, and the supports are slightly tapered. They take the place of classical columns,

the joints represent the capitals, the side view of the steel panel appears like classical beams, the compartments on the lower side look like a cassette-type ceiling.

Mies van der Rohe was given a high degree of planning freedom, mainly because the public demand that the world-famous architect should be represented by a building in Berlin had been the original reason for the project. The 8.50 metre high hall which was built below the largest free-spanning steel panel in the world (with two installation shafts without load-bearing properties in the interior) is set on a stone terrace, and the actual museum storey is below the terrace. It opens up to the west with a large glass facade looking out onto an outdoor sculpture courtyard surrounded by walls.

Post-war Modernism West
Ludwig Mies van der Rohe 1965–68
Tiergarten, Kulturforum, Potsdamer Strasse 50
Open: Tues, Weds, Fri 10–18 hrs., Thurs 10–22 hrs., Sat–Sun 11–18 hrs.,
Tel. 26 60
www.smb.museum
▷ Bus M29, 148

Staatsbibliothek Haus 2
(State Library Building 2)

The "Kulturforum" planned by Hans Scharoun envisaged the Philharmonie (cf. p. 166f.), the "Kammermusiksaal" (Chamber music hall), the Institute for Music Research, six museums and one guest house. But the original plans were never implemented – the idea of an architecturally coherent ensemble was given up when Mies van der Rohe was commissioned to build the Neue Nationalgalerie (cf. p. 168f.). The competition declared in 1964 for a state library on Potsdamer Strasse (as a replacement for the old state library which was in former East Berlin) was again won by Hans Scharoun. Building work began in 1967, and after Scharoun's death in 1972 the project was continued by his associate Edgar Wisniewski.

The elongated high structure of the archive with its yellow anodised aluminium panels rises above several lower buildings and reflects the exterior appearance of the Philharmonie. In front of it are the reading and lecture rooms, foyers, administration rooms and the attached Ibero-American institute, which are situated in separate granite-faced buildings.

This varied and colourful exterior corresponds to the complex but generously proportioned interior. The reading room below the uniform flat roof alleviated by glass pyramids and skylights is subdivided into various areas on different levels. The balconies, stairs and galleries create a varied "reading landscape".

Like the Philharmonie, the state library is also a radical contrast – and topographical confrontation – to the Neue Nationalgalerie by Mies van der Rohe. Whereas Mies designed an "archetypal hall" with a generally valid form, Scharoun created the state library as a building which was improvised rather than perfected and which "left scope for development". Whereas Mies, who had spent the National Socialist period in exile in America, set the clear structure of his buildings against the chaos of the environment, Scharoun had survived this period by building single family houses in Germany. As the first city building councillor appointed by the Soviets

from 1945–46, he used decentralised, loose structures and planned chaos as a weapon against the neo-classicism of Albert Speer. He wanted the human being to become the standard by which everything was judged.

In 1968, Rolf Gutbrod was commissioned with the construction of the other museums in the Kulturforum, but after violent criticism of his concept and his first completed building, the "Kunstgewerbemuseum" (Museum of Arts and Crafts), a new competition was declared in 1985. The prizewinners Christoph Sattler and Heinz Hilmer constructed the other buildings in the museum complex: the "Kupferstichkabinett" (Copper engraving museum), the "Kunstbibliothek" (Art library) and the "Gemäldegalerie" (Paintings gallery).

Post-war Modernism West
Hans Scharoun, Edgar Wisniewski 1967–78
Tiergarten, Kulturforum, Potsdamer Strasse 33
Open: Mon–Fri 9–21 hrs., Sat 9–19 hrs., Tel. 26 60
www.staatsbibliothek-berlin.de
▷ S / U Potsdamer Platz, bus M29, 148

Fernsehturm (Television Tower)

It is a strange idea to build a 365 metre high television tower in the middle of a city. It is so unusual that the tower in Berlin is even today the only television tower in such a central position in Europe, and perhaps in the whole world. The local people have not just become accustomed to it – it soon became the pride of the people of East Berlin, and it is now one of the undisputed major landmarks of the unified city. Hardly anyone in Berlin finds it out of place.

The idea of building such a television tower grew out of the need for a separate television broadcasting system for the eastern part of the city. Various projects outside the city had been rejected, and when even the tower block planned on the site of the demolished palace in the typical wedding-cake style of contemporary Moscow and Warsaw became obsolete, it was decided to implement this unusual project. It was carried out in 1965–69 by the collective of Günther Kollmann.

There is a legend that the height was prescribed by Walter Ulbricht so that every school child could remember it: 365 metres, one for every day of the year. It was the second tallest tower in Europe, surpassed only by the television tower in Moscow.

The reinforced concrete shaft reaches up to a height of 250 metres, and above it is a red and white striped steel mast. In 1997 the top end was removed and replaced by a tip that is three metres higher.

The sphere on the tower covers seven storeys, two of which are open to the public: the viewing floor at a height of 203 metres and above it the Telecafé in which the outer ring with the tables revolved around its own axis once per hour. A few years ago, the rotation time was reduced to half an hour to shorten the amount of time spent there by guests. The exterior surface of the sphere consists of 140 stainless steel segments, and when the sun shines a large cross appears as a reflection. When the SED

communist party was in power, this was jokingly referred to as "God's revenge".

The buildings around the base of the tower were added from 1969–72, planned by the collective of Walter Herzog. The two storey exhibition and restaurant building is concealed beneath a roof that appears to have been folded together and opened up again. The ensemble is completed by cascades, water fountains and the enormous Neptune fountain which was once situated on the palace square as a "gift to the Emperor from the city of Berlin" (Reinhold Begas 1888–91) and which personified four German rivers of the period, the Rhine, Elbe, Oder and Weichsel.

Post-war Modernism East
Collective Günther Kollmann and others 1965–69, Surrounding buildings: collective Walter Herzog and others 1969–72
Mitte, Alexanderplatz, Panoramastrasse 1a
Open: daily 10–24 hrs., Tel. 24 75 75 37
www.tv-turm.de
▷ S / U Alexanderplatz

ICC – Internationales Congress Centrum (ICC – International Congress Centre)

Success is relative. Opened in 1979, the International Congress Centre (ICC) Berlin has become by far the most important congress centre in Germany and one of the busiest in the world. The company in charge of the fairgrounds is very proud that it has been voted the world's favourite congress centre several times. Two large and several slightly smaller halls and spaces make it Europe's largest congress centre – and yet it is still considered too small, too uneconomical in its layout, too expensive in its operating costs – and, in addition, the centre is contaminated with asbestos. Following many long discussions about its possible demolition and the construction of a new structure, it will be renovated and is intended to be self-supporting by 2016.

The design by Ralf Schüler and Ursulina Schüler-Witte won the competition for a new multifunctional hall in 1965. The requirements changed numerous times and, by the time construction began in 1975, what had once been a simple hall had become the largest and most expensive construction project in post-war Germany.

The building site, a traffic island situated between the highway and two roads, Messedamm and Kantstrasse, gave the Schülers the idea of designing the building like a ship with different decks. Three basement levels are located beneath the street and house the supply centres. The basement structure is penetrated by two rows of thirteen round supports with a diameter of 2.50 metres, the top of which – via the distribution level on the ground floor – are equipped with elastomer bearings, which are rubberlike bodies that prevent the transfer of sound and vibrations. These, in turn, support reinforced concrete girders between which the smaller halls are situated. Located above these, approximately 13 metres above street level, are the two larger halls, which, when combined with the middle stage, create a large space with 9100 seats. The wall and ceiling construction that surrounds the entire construction supports a steel lattice framework to which the exte-

rior-lying staircases are mounted. Sound and vibrations between the staircases and the framework are insulated using neoprene bearings. Jean Ipoustéguy's bronze sculpture, "Alexander d. Gr. vor Ekbatana," is situated in front of the main facade of the 320-metre-long and 80-metre-wide futuristic building, which, as an analogy to a ship, has a continuous glass (ship's) bridge.

The Schülers also designed the curious "Bierpinsel" (beer brush) in Steglitz, a 46-metre-high tower, which houses a restaurant and is faced with bright red plastic cladding; it is a prime example of 1970s Pop Architecture. Also located in Steglitz is the most famous example of nepotism-sponsored monumental architecture from the same year: the office building, "Steglitzer Kreisel" (Sigrid Kressmann-Zschach 1969–72), which is 119 metres high and still the highest structure in West Berlin.

Modernism
Ralf Schüler, Ursulina Schüler-Witte 1973–79
Charlottenburg, Messedamm 22
Open: for events, Tel. 30 69 69 69
▷ U Kaiserdamm, S Witzleben

Bauhaus-Archiv – Museum für Gestaltung (Bauhaus Archive – Museum of Design)

To create a building in a style appropriate for the Bauhaus Archive when it moved to Berlin in 1971, it was decided to use a design by the school's founder and first director, Walter Gropius, who died two years previously – a design which had originally been created for the northern slope of the Rosenhöhe in Darmstadt in 1964. Gropius' former associate Alexander Cvijanovic modified it for the location in Berlin. For example, the ramp which cuts through the complex was added by Cvijanovic.

The complex consists of two two-storey structures of almost equal length with different ground layouts which are set slightly offset and parallel to each other and which are linked by an intermediate section. The characteristic features are the rows of 4 by 4 metre high roof hoods which are strictly aligned to face north (for the best illumination of the exhibits). By contrast with the design by Gropius the facade, which is mounted on a reinforced concrete framework, is divided into small individual sections by dark joints between the white painted concrete panels. The northern sections contains the administrative and working rooms, and the southern section contains the exhibition rooms. The coloured metal columns at both ends of the ramp are by Max Bill.

The task of the archive is to collect the legacy of one of the most important colleges of art of the 20th century, to organise it scientifically and present it to the public. The state school, founded in 1919 in Weimar by Walter Gropius, moved to Dessau in 1925 and was closed in 1932 following the NSDAP's victory in the municipal council. Ludwig Mies van der Rohe, who had been the school's director since 1930, ran the school as a private institution for another six months in Berlin in an unmaintained factory building on Birkbuschstrasse in Lankwitz.

Walter Gropius designed a series of buildings in Berlin, although his name is most closely associated with the housing development "Großsiedlung Britz-Buckow-Rudow," which was renamed

Gropiusstadt in 1972. It was from Gropius's office, "The Architects Collaborative," that the original plans came, but these were greatly modified under the direction of Gropius's contact architect, Wils Ebert. Gropius's most famous house, the wooden Villa Sommerfeld, was destroyed but a similar structure, the Haus Otte (1921 / 22) on Zehlendorf's Wolzogenstrasse, still exists.

The area around the Bauhaus Archive was heavily damaged during World War II. Buildings to have survived the war in direct vicinity are the Villa von der Heydt (1862), an imposing classical urban villa and the Estonian Embassy on Hildebrandstrasse. On the southern bank of the Landwehrkanal is the monumental Grand Hotel Esplanade (Jürgen Sawade 1986–88).

Post-war Modernism West
Walter Gropius / Alexander Cvijanovic 1976–79
Tiergarten, Klingelhöferstrasse 14
Open: Weds–Mon 10–17 hrs., Tel. 254 00 20
www.bauhaus.de
▷ Bus 100, M29

Friedrichstadtpalast
(Friedrichstadt Palace Theatre)

The Friedrichstadtpalast was built from 1981–84 and is the most prominent example of GDR post-modernism and one of the highlights of the slab construction method. By contrast with the facade of the ambitious Weston Grand Hotel Unter den Linden which draws on the rich ornamentation of Berlin classicism and the new buildings on Gendarmenmarkt which translate Art Nouveau elements into the formal language of slab construction, a completely new ornamentation style was found for the facade of the Friedrichstadtpalast.

The largest revue theatre in Europe has a name rich in tradition. Between Friedrichstrasse and the present Berliner Ensemble, in the street Am Zirkus, was the famous preceding building which developed from a market hall built in 1865–68 which was later converted for use as a circus. In 1919 the theatre specialist Max Reinhardt took over the building and had it converted by Hans Poelzig to the famous "Tropfsteinhöhle" (dripstone cave) which compensated for the great acoustic and design problems of the building by its Expressionist decor. In 1924, Erik Charell's revue theatre moved in, and from 1933 it was known as "Theater des Volkes" (theatre of the people) with an emphasis on Berlin operetta.

Before the end of 1945 the building was again used as an entertainment theatre, and from 1947 it bore the present name. Fluctuations in the groundwater level put an end to the enormous structure which was built on wooden piles. Because of the rotting wooden supports, it had to close down in 1980 and was pulled down in 1986.

The centre of the new palace theatre building is the large auditorium for an audience of 1900 which is equipped with all the technical finery including a lift platform with a diameter of 12 metres on the front part of the stage. In the southern part of the building is the "Kleine Revue" (small revue theatre) with 240 seats, and the rehearsal rooms are in the rear part of the building. The complete

exterior shell is clad with sandstone-coloured concrete slabs, the foyer block is decorated on Friedrichstrasse with multicoloured glass concrete elements which are appropriate for a revue theatre with a light entertainment programme.

To the south of the Spree is a further centre of light entertainment, the former "Admiralspalast" (Admiral's palace) with its bombastic facade design. It was built in 1910 as a pleasure building with a luxurious indoor swimming bath and ice skating hall, and after several alterations it now contains a theatre hall with 1750 seats (where the ice skating hall once was, 1955–1997 "Metropol theatre") and the cabaret "Die Distel" (in the front building). Nearby, three plush and splendid theatre halls in the Historicism style – the Berliner Ensemble, the Deutsche Theater and the Komische Oper – have retained their interiors.

Post-modernism East
Collective of Walter Schwarz and others 1981–84
Mitte, Friedrichstrasse 107
www.friedrichstadtpalast.de
▷ S / U Friedrichstrasse, U Oranienburger Tor

Nikolaiviertel (Nikolai District)

There are a number of towns and cities in Germany in which the mediaeval centre was destroyed in the Second World War, but very few have cleared away the old town as completely as Berlin. In the area of the ancient town centre, a Socialist city centre arose with large residential blocks, large areas of greenery, large main roads and, not least, a television tower (cf. p. 172f.) in the middle. The older buildings that survived or were restored actually originated from later periods in which the old town buildings had also been treated with little respect, and in some cases whole districts had been pulled down, as in the example of the "Rotes Rathaus" and the "Stadthaus".

Only the original heart of Berlin, the area around the Nikolaikirche (cf. p. 16f.) where the first merchants settled in the 12th century near the crossing point over the Spree, was initially spared – the ruins of the church and the few remaining residential buildings were left to their fate into the 1970s. But for the 750 year celebrations in Berlin in 1987, it was decided that the old heart of Berlin should be "formed into a harmonious unit in accordance with its historical significance with new, reconstructed and restored buildings, streets and squares, by means of construction, spatial design and artistic measures, in such a way that the living reference to the original state and the rich tradition of Berlin's history should always be accessible to everyday experience".

On the basis of plans by the collective of Günter Stahn, which was the prizewinner in the urban development competition of 1979, Berlin thus acquired a historicised but unhistoric semblance of an old town.

Around the "honestly" restored Nikolaikirche replicas of old buildings were created, "adaptations of old Berlin citizen houses", including "Berlin's oldest pub" the "Nussbaum" (Nut tree) which had formerly been on Fischerinsel (Fishers' island), the "Gerichtslaube" (small court building) dating from the 13th century which

was pulled down in 1860 and rebuilt practically as a neo-Gothic new building in the palace park in Babelsberg, the picturesque row of buildings to the south of the Nikolaikirche and "Berlin's most beautiful corner", the Ephraim-Palais (cf. p. 48f.) on Molkenmarkt.

Other buildings that have been rebuilt include three historical residential and shopping buildings, including the splendid "Kurfürstenhaus" (Electoral house) on Kupfergraben (1895 by Carl Gause) and the baroque Knoblauchhaus with its early classical style facade. The old ensemble is enclosed between three to eight storey slab concrete buildings with apartments, shops and restaurants.

Gothic / Classicism / Historicism / Post-modernism
Collectives of Günter Stahn, Heinz Mehlan, Rolf Ricken (reconstructions)
1979–87
Mitte
▷ S / U Alexanderplatz, U Klosterstrasse, bus 100

IBA-Bauten am Fraenkelufer
(IBA Buildings on Fraenkelufer)

The year 1979 was a year of upheaval in (West) German architectural history. When the International Building Exhibition (IBA) was constituted, this was not only the beginning of post-modernism, it also represented a change of paradigm – away from demolition and complete redevelopment to a more careful urban renewal. The aim was to regain "the inner city as a place to live in".

By contrast with its predecessor in 1957, the IBA 1987 formed an umbrella for various individual projects in Kreuzberg, Tiergarten and Tegel. A relatively small but much acclaimed project was the closing of a vacant plot in a block on Fraenkelufer in Kreuzberg in a part of the city which suffered less from war damage, but rather from post-war planning.

It is in the shadow of one of the most infamous redevelopment areas in Berlin, the tower block development at Kottbusser Tor known as the "Neues Kreuzberger Zentrum".

Even between Kottbusser Tor and Fraenkelufer the complete demolition of the old buildings was planned. The area near the canal was to become a green zone, an urban motorway from Hasenheide was to lead across Wassertorplatz to Oranienplatz. This questionable concept was only finally rejected in 1976.

The old buildings on Fraenkelufer were preserved and two gaps were closed with "gatehouses". They lead into the centre of the block, where a further building block arose against the opposite fire wall. The designs were by the couple Hinrich and Inken Baller who developed their own, unmistakable style. Their facades are characterised by projecting lines in the balconies, eaves and roof dormers. Elements of Art Nouveau, Expressionism and Modernism are whimsically integrated, but without degenerating into a superficial randomness.

The apartments are also imaginative and varied in their floor layout, with the sizes ranging from two room to six room flats, including maisonettes. But the building costs were still low, and

the buildings were part of the subsidised public building scheme. Other notable buildings by Hinrich and Inken Baller can be found at Kottbusser Damm 2–3, on Schlossstrasse in Charlottenburg (double sports hall and residential building) and in Dahlem (Philosophical Institute of the Free University).

At Admiralstrasse 16, a much acclaimed "self-building project" arose in the context of the IBA. Here, a reinforced concrete framework was set into a gap between buildings, and on the six storeys the future tenants were able to insert their own individually designed flats in consultation with the architect.

Post-modernism
Hinrich and Inken Baller 1982–84
Kreuzberg, Fraenkelufer
▷ U Kottbusser Tor, U Schönleinstrasse

Wohnpark am ehemaligen Berlin-Museum (Residential Park on the former Berlin-Museum)

The core areas of the International Building Exhibition 1987 were the post-war wasteland areas in Kreuzberg, which were now carefully developed. One of the most interesting projects in this area, which extends almost from Potsdamer Platz in the west to Moritzplatz in the east, is on Lindenstrasse. In the first competition declared by the IBA in 1980, the aim was to integrate two old buildings – Berlin-Museum (today Jewish Museum) and the Victoria insurance building – into an overall urban development concept. The prize-winners were Hans Kollhoff and Arthur Ovaska, but as so often in competitions their original concept was completely changed, especially by private developers. Instead of a closed block development in the typical Berlin style, a number of individual buildings, mainly so-called "town villas", were built from 1984–86 designed by eight teams of architects from Germany, Switzerland, Austria, the Czech Republic and Japan. The project was thus similar to the project on Rauchstrasse (south of the Tiergarten), but without reaching its "space-creating" quality.

The entrance building by Werner Kreis and the brothers Ulrich and Peter Schaad drew much criticism. It was meant to mediate between the two old buildings and to shield the inner area of the town villas from Lindenstrasse. Instead, with its bulky smoothness and the arch-like roof structure it rather overpowers the delicate baroque building. The twelve axially arranged villas, amongst which the northern row is interlinked, are fairly small in size and adorned with post-modernist elements. On Alte Jakobstrasse the development is completed by a long block by the Czech Stavoprojekt Liberec.

On the block behind the Victoria insurance building, Kollhoff and Ovaska built a residential block with a length of 170 metres with a "classically modern" formal language, and the development along the northern and eastern edge of the block is by Dieter Frowein and Gerhard Spangenberg. At the centre of the block,

integrated into the court complex of the Victoria building, is a proto-
typical post-modernist building by Arata Isozaki.

Not far to the north are two other IBA development areas: Rit-
terstrasse South, developed from 1979–81 based on a concept by
Rob Krier and consisting of heterogeneous buildings with post-
modernist facades designed by various architects, and Ritter-
strasse North, built from 1982–88 also based on a master plan by
Krier. This large complex, which appears homogeneous despite
the individual styles of different architects, is grouped around
Schinkelplatz, on which stands the classical-style "Feilner-Haus",
a (vehemently criticised) new building by Krier.

A stunning example of Post Modern architecture is the redevelopment of the Tegel Industrial Harbor, built in 1985–88 for the International Building Exhibition (IBA) according to a master plan by the
Californian firm Moore, Ruble and Yudell.

Post-modernism / Modernism
Hans Kollhoff, Arthur Ovaska and others 1984–86
Kreuzberg, Lindenstrasse / Am Berlin-Museum
▷ U Hallesches Tor, U Kochstrasse, bus M29

Kant-Dreieck (Kant Triangle) and Ludwig-Erhard-Haus (Ludwig Erhard Building)

"The large 'cockscomb' of riveted metal sheeting which crowns the building and rotates with the wind is a greeting in the various directions and even into the past: it greets the writers in the 'Romanisches Café' and the artists of the secession, it flirts with Josephine Baker and the stage of the Theater des Westens. The Kant triangle aims to corre- spond symbolically to this location where melancholy and cheerfulness are balanced."

This is a demanding expectation which Josef Paul Kleihues places on his building, and whether the architecture matches his claims is a subject for debate. But one thing is certain: with the large "sail" 36 metres above ground level, the West Berlin city acquired a new landmark – and Kleihues won the architecture prize of the Association of German Architects in 1994.

The lower section of the complex consists of two cubes with edges of 18 metres. The lower five-storey cube is faced with gneiss slate panels with a simplicity typical of Kleihues, as is the adjacent triangular structure with a large facade facing Fasanenstrasse. The top six-storey cube is a steel structure with external diagonal trusses. Originally the building was planned to be one cube taller, but the district council refused building permission. That means that the unproportionally squat dimensions are no fault of Klei-hues. At present, discussions are being held on the possibility of making the building taller after all.

Across the road is the extension building of the Chamber of Commerce and Industry (IHK) by Nicholas Grimshaw, the "Ludwig-Erhard-Haus", which was only completed in 1998 but which was already used by the Berlin stock market from 1997 (photo). The structure was modelled on the armadillo, and the shape of its shell is picked up by the high curved steel beams. The underlying idea was to create an adequate, organic architectural framework for the living "organism" of the stock market which changes on a day to day basis. Originally the curved steel beams were also

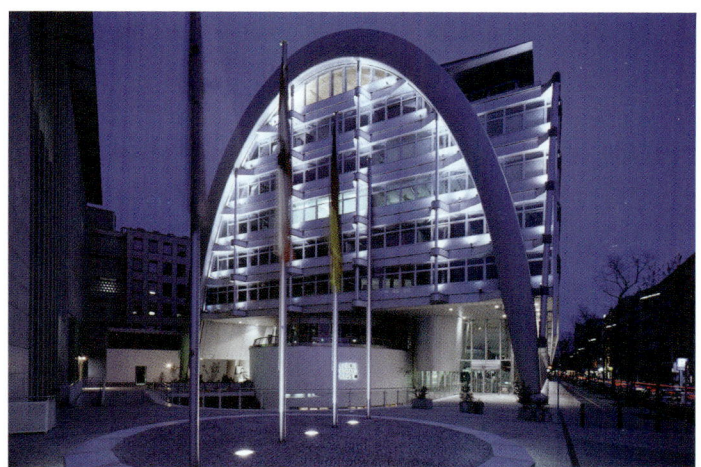

designed as the facade facing Fasanenstrasse, but the building now has a smooth vertical five storey facade to ensure that the eaves height can be seen – this, too, was a requirement of the building authorities.

The interior has an inside street which is open to the public and provides a view of the stock market trading room. There are also two glass-covered atriums as high as the buildings between the flexibly arranged offices.

Therefore, two buildings based on animal forms are situated opposite each other with contrasting architectural styles: on the one hand the "cockscomb" on the strictly rational design of the Kant triangle, on the other hand the expressive shell of the "armadillo", an unusual feat of engineering, although the facade design was not able to maintain the same standard.

Contemporary Modernism
Kant triangle: Josef Paul Kleihues 1992–95; Ludwig-Erhard-Haus: Nicholas Grimshaw 1994–98
Charlottenburg, Kantstrasse 155 / Fasanenstrasse 83 / 84
▷ S / U Zoologischer Garten, U Kurfürstendamm

Willy-Brandt-Haus (Willy Brandt Building)

The Willy Brandt building was dedicated in 1996 as the first newly built party headquarters in Berlin. The location in the old workers' district of Kreuzberg was symbolic.

The architectural challenge lay not only in the pointed shape of the land, but also in the desolate urban setting. Due to the heavy destruction in the Second World War, there are still many waste areas and a number of post-war buildings without any development context, and nearby is the restructured Mehringplatz which is unsuccessful from today's perspective (built up to 1975 to plans by Hans Scharoun, modified by Werner Düttmann).

In this disparate environment, the SPD national headquarters built in 1993–96 to plans by the Wiesbaden architect Helge Bofinger sets a striking tone. The dominant element of the seven storey building is naturally the blunted corner of the block. Above the concave ground layout, the upper three storeys project forwards. Sixth floor balconies which project obliquely out of the alignment lines of the side facades create an additional dynamism and at the same time evoke the bridge of a steamer – symbolic of the fact that the "captain of the ship", the party chairman, has his office in the adjacent room.

The exterior is characterised by large window areas which are set in a wide grid of light-coloured limestone panels. At the centre of the building is an atrium with a full glass roof spanning the height of the building, which is also used for cultural events. In the rear section, an arcade passes through the building. On the ground floor there are shops and restaurants.

With the clear lines and dynamism of the building and the transparency of his facades, Bofinger follows on from the tradition of classical modernism. The Willy Brandt building can be compared in quality with the famous IG-Metall building by Erich Mendelsohn (1929 / 30) which is on a similarly structured plot the other side of Mehringplatz (Alte Jakobstrasse 148–155).

Contemporary Modernism
Helge Bofinger 1993–96
Kreuzberg, Wilhelmstrasse 141 / corner of Stresemannstrasse
Exhibitions: Thurs–Sun 12–18 hrs., Tel. 25 99 37 00
www.willy-brandt-haus.de
▷ U Hallesches Tor, bus M41

Friedrichstadt-Passagen
(Friedrichstadt Shopping Arcades)

Of the numerous new building projects along Friedrichstrasse, the three blocks of the "Friedrichstadt-Passagen" were the first and the most noted. The planning and development of the area had already begun during the last few years of the GDR, but after a new competition the unfinished buildings were pulled down again at the beginning of the 1990s. This group of buildings derives its name from the arcade of shops which links the three complexes below street level.

The southernmost building, Quartier 205, is the only one to cover an entire block of streets, which means that it also has an effect on Gendarmenmarkt to the rear. Here, Oswald Mathias Ungers takes as his motif the subject of the "Berlin block structure". Around an eight storey core building which opens up to two inner courtyards, six "individual" buildings are grouped which are aligned around the edge of the block and, with six storeys, follow the eaves height of the surrounding buildings. In the recesses between them are the entrances to the arcades which run all through the building, and the recesses also reveal the core building with its different coloured cladding. It remains open to discussion whether the smooth stone facades and the basic concept of a structure based solely on the square without any adornments is sufficient for the development of such a large block building.

An extreme contrast is the neighbouring block by the American Henry Cobb (photo). The facade is characterised by wedge-like projecting elements which stand out above the eaves cornice and are strikingly illuminated at night. The restless style of noble materials in expressive forms is continued in the interior. In his own words, Cobb wanted to demonstrate "that a large commercial development can nevertheless be so designed that the urban scene is not suppressed, but enlivened."

The northern block designed by the French architect Jean Nouvel for the department store Galeries Lafayette (in the fore-

front of the photograph) was best received by architectural critics. By contrast with the stone architecture demanded by the city building director Stimmann, the exterior surface consists entirely of glass. However, it is not designed to be transparent. Above the horizontally structured facade, high rooftop elements rise. The main entrance is strangely inconspicuous, and there is an even smaller side entrance on Französische Strasse. In the interior there are two enormous cones covered in plexiglas instead of an inner courtyard. The lost sales space is compensated for by low ceilings, which means that the general spatial impression is not generous.

All blocks are used for shops, offices and apartments.

Contemporary Modernism / Post-modernism
Oswald Mathias Ungers, Henry Cobb, Jean Nouvel 1993–96
Mitte, Friedrichstrasse
▷ U Französische Strasse, U Stadtmitte

Quartier Schützenstrasse

A "Quartier", one of the large street blocks in the rectangular grid of the Friedrichstadt district, need not be developed in the same style as the buildings erected along Friedrichstrasse – as is demonstrated by the "Quartier Schützenstrasse" situated between Schützenstrasse, Markgrafenstrasse, Zimmerstrasse and Charlottenstrasse. Here, close to the former border between East and West Berlin, only one building survived the war and the postwar period, the remainder of the block was waste land.

The design by Aldo Rossi (with M. Kocher and M. Scheurer, planning partners: Götz Bellmann and Walter Böhm) decided against a monolith block structure, and broke the block down into numerous plots, some of which were based on the pre-war buildings. By using different facade and roof designs, each plot has a different visual character, but to enable the property to be flexibly let, the entire block was constructed with equal floor heights so that in the interior it is possible to combine rooms behind several facades into a single suite. But that is the only feature that shows that the block was designed and built as a unit.

Besides the outer block structure, the architects also revived the typical old Berlin rear courtyard building principle and created four inner courtyards, which again are enclosed by rear facades of different design. Here, however, the facade facing the rear courtyard sometimes does not correspond with the outer facade design, which further underlines the extravagance of the block frontage.

The facade designs emphasise the uniform concept. Rossi and his partners did not try to create a copy of a Berlin residential block from the age of industrial expansion, rather they aimed to create a modern version with historical references, but with unmistakably modern forms and materials. Especially the bright colours of some of the buildings and facade sections create a completely innovative element in the inner city of Berlin.

A special humorous touch on Schützenstrasse is the copy of the

Palazzo Farnese, a famous Roman Renaissance building by Antonio da Sangallo the younger and Michelangelo, which stands out from the overall consistency of the block design with its high round windows and the thick roof cornice.

The "Quartier Schützenstrasse" is certainly the most extraordinary block development in the area around Friedrichstrasse and the former strip of the Berlin Wall. Whether it is successful and represents a real alternative to the large block areas and "box-type architecture" that dominate the new appearance of the centre of Berlin – that is a decision that each reader must make for himself.

A similar building, also consisting of various small sections but without quite such brightly coloured facades, is the ensemble "New Hackescher Markt," built 1996–98 by Götz Bellmann and Walter Böhm – the same Berlin architects who were involved in building the "Quartier Schützenstrasse."

Post-modernism
Aldo Rossi, M. Kocher, M. Scheurer, Götz Bellmann, Walter Böhm 1995–98
Mitte, Schützenstrasse
▷ U Kochstrasse, U Stadtmitte, U Spittelmarkt, bus M29

Jüdisches Museum / Libeskindbau
(Jewish Museum / Libeskind Building)

The task for a competition was to design an extension building for the Berlin-Museum which could also accommodate the Jewish department. The prizewinner among the 165 entrants was the American Daniel Libeskind. Next to the high quality baroque building of the former Appeal Court, which was built in 1734–35 to plans by Philipp Gerlach, he placed an irregularly angled, shining silver solitary building as a complete stylistic break without any exterior connection.

"The idea is very simple: to build a museum around an emptiness which runs through it, an emptiness which must be experienced by the visitor. In material terms, very little is left of the Jewish presence in Berlin – small items, documents, archive material, which evoke absence rather than presence." Correspondingly, the American born in Poland designed a monolith shaped like bolt of lightning on the proposed triangular plot, with a silver metal outer skin marked by numerous cuts, like scratches and injuries. The only common element with the old building is that both are the same height.

The ground layout, which is not subjected to any rational scheme, is cut through by an east-west axis. These cut-through spaces which are as high as the building can not be entered, they can only be crossed on bridges. They symbolise the "emptiness" which the extermination of the Jews left in Berlin. Within the individual storeys there are no other sub-divisions.

The Jewish Museum is entered below ground level from the old building. A long straight staircase leads up to the second storey, and another staircase at the other end of the building leads to the first floor, thus making it possible to tour the whole museum. The third storey is reserved for the administration.

The Libeskind building impressively shows that "Deconstructivism", which seems to overcome the laws of structural analysis, is not just an architectural fashion but can also be a coherent form

of expression. The building has been showered with advance praise – among architectural critics Libeskind's museum is probably the most positively received new building of the 1990s in Berlin.

In 2007 the interior courtyard of the old building was roofed over according to a plan of Libeskind. An extension is planned on the other side of Lindenstrasse as the Jewish Museum, which houses the largest exhibit of Jewish history in Europe, is one of the most-visited museums in Berlin. Even before its opening in 2001 it was removed from the Association of Municipal Museums and was transferred to a municipal foundation.

Deconstructivism
Daniel Libeskind 1993–99
Kreuzberg, Lindenstrasse 9–14
Open: Tues–Sun 10–20 hrs., Mo 10–22 hrs., Tel. 25 99 33 00
www.jmberlin.de
▷ U Hallesches Tor, U Kochstrasse, bus M29, 265

Potsdamer Platz / Daimler City

The city planners seem to have been right after all. The people of Berlin have welcomed the cafés, cinemas and large shopping complex of the new Daimler city with open arms. On an area of 16.8 acres between Potsdamer Platz and Reichpietschufer, a whole new urban district has come into existence. The master plan was designed by the prizewinners Renzo Piano and Christoph Kohlbecker, and five other teams of architects or individual architects were brought in to carry out the detailed planning. This ensured that the new district would have a certain homogeneity and, at the same time, architectural variety.

From Potsdamer Platz, the visitor enters the district as if through a city gate. Two tower buildings by Piano / Kohlbecker (left) and Hans Kollhoff (right) frame the Alte Potsdamer Strasse, which here again follows its pre-war line. On the right, the visitor passes the building blocks by Lauber & Wöhr and José Rafael Moneo (Hotel Hyatt), on the left the Weinhaus Huth, the only surviving old building, and the shopping mall which is framed on the street side by buildings by Piano / Kohlbecker and Richard Rogers (facing Link-strasse). The focal point of the complex is Marlene-Dietrich-Platz (photo), which is dominated by the double building of the casino and the musical theatre with its large roof (Piano / Kohlbecker).

Piano and Kohlbecker also designed the Debis headquarters by the Landwehrkanal. The glass-roofed atrium extends through the middle of the 163 metre long block, and the buildings at the side rise in three steps by one storey at a time, thus leading gradually to the tower building as the end building. The south and west facade of this 85 metre high glass office tower have a second curtain-type facade for energy conservation purposes.

The atrium is open to the public. The interior block structure is broken up at several points by staircases and balcony shafts, and the wall surfaces are enlivened by louvers. In the basement, high

arcades open to auxiliary rooms which are used for the cafeteria and shops.

Next to the building are the eight storey office buildings by Arata Isozaki and Steffen Lehmann, connected by bridges in the upper three storeys. The smooth facades are dominated by the change from red to lilac-brown ceramic tiles and the trapezoidal windows.

Leipziger Platz, designed as an octagon in 1734, has been in the process of reconstruction since 1995. The Berlin Senate required developers to face all building facades in a tripartite arrangement with traditional light natural stone. The four attic floors above the 22-metre-high pediment are reserved for apartments. Still unclear is how the enormous complex, which once housed the Wertheim department store will be used.

Contemporary Architecture
Renzo Piano, Christoph Kohlbecker (master plan and individual buildings), Arata Isozaki / Steffen Lehmann, Hans Kollhoff, Lauber & Wöhr, José Rafael Moneo, Richard Rogers 1994–99
Tiergarten, Reichpietschufer
▷ S / U Potsdamer Platz, bus M29, M41

GSW-Hochhaus (GSW High-Rise)

They are building high-rises again in Berlin. One of the most striking new examples is the highly acclaimed central administration
building of the GSW housing property association located on Kochstrasse in Kreuzberg. The architects, Matthias Sauerbruch and
Louisa Hutton, also designed the iridescent Photonic Centre at the
Adlershof scholarly institute, also known as the "Amoeba", – a
successful show piece of Berlin nineties architecture.

The GSW building, a 22 storey, long and very narrow high-rise,
could have turned out ungainly, but the architects cleverly
achieved the contrary effect: they placed the light steel and glass
construction on two flat pedestals that – with their black slate-like
facade and horizontally placed windows – create a strong contrast. The building and pedestals are slightly concave and the
"winged roof," a design popular from the fifties, atop the 85 metre
high construction gives the impression it might spread its wings
and take off at any moment. But the best feature is the double-
layered energy-saving facade, which covers the surface in flicker-
ing iridescence, the colours changing with increasing intensity as
one approaches the building. The various pale red tones of the
shimmering lamella panels which cover each window and protect
against the sun create a mosaic facade, which for Berlin is one-of-
a-kind.

Fresh air constantly flows into the one metre wide space beneath
the facade, is warmed and rises upward, pulling the stale air out
of the offices and achieving an energy-saving effect of about 40
percent. The aerodynamic low pressure is produced by the large
wind sail on the roof.

At the backside awaits the next surprise: The high-rise conceals
to the west an unattached 17 storey building, whose right-angled
frame construction reveals its post-war origins. It is interesting
how subtly each individual building element is linked to the next:
The elevator and stairwell tower is located at the back and covered

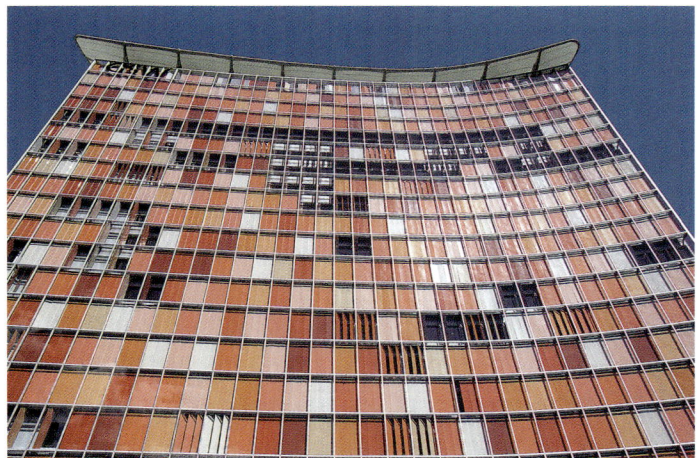

with the same black plates that were used to encase the pedestals. A narrow glass tract leads from there to the older building.

Of a completely different character is a four-storey oval-shaped construction with winding bands of windows that is set upon the back section of the flat building on Kochstrasse. Its corrugated iron outer-casing shimmers in various radiant tones. An ensemble is thus achieved which reflects the architectural disunity of the environs but which also harmoniously connects the very contrasting building elements into a successful synthesis.

New building: Contemporary Modernism
Matthias Sauerbruch, Louisa Hutton 1995–99
Old building: Post-war Modernism
Paul Schwebes, Hans Schoszberger 1960 / 61
Kreuzberg, Kochstrasse
▷ U Kochstrasse, bus M29

DZ Bank on Pariser Platz

The architect Frank O. Gehry is extremely popular with developers. He not only guarantees a strictly maintained cost framework, but also a broad echo in the media. Gehry is one of the undisputed stars of the architectural scene. The architect, who was born in 1929 in Toronto and has long lived in California, became famous in 1978. Tired of building interminable shopping malls, he served notice on his client and converted his bourgeois suburban single family house into a wild conglomeration of corrugated iron, chipboard and wire netting with a tilted glass cube above the kitchen. "Deconstructivism" was born, and Gehry's house became a pilgrimage site for a new generation of architects.

Since then, Gehry has lived out his child-like joy in form. His buildings provoke, are completely out of the ordinary or cause offence, but never out of mere sensationalism: the formal escapades are always earthed in careful workmanship and functional aptness. Technically, this architecture is possible because of the use of the computer which calculates the parts necessary for the building so that they fit accurately.

Compared with Gehry's previous buildings, the Guggenheim Museum in Bilbao, the residential house "Ginger und Fred" in Prague and the Zollhof in Düsseldorf, the Berlin bank building – almost predictably – is the least spectacular, at least from the outside. That is particularly due to the strict regulations which the architects had to follow on Pariser Platz. The requirement of opening the facade with a wall-to-window ratio of 50:50 was solved by Gehry in a surprising way: he combined the stone areas to a pillar-like shape, and between them he placed the windows which are held merely by narrow window breasts. Thus, the facade reflects the basic form of Brandenburg Gate. Its special feature is the sloping orientation of the windows on the ground floor and the fourth floor.

The rectangular plot is completely built over. At its centre is an

inner courtyard which is covered by a complicated glass structure, clad with wood and surrounded by offices. This is the where the most spectacular element of the building is situated: a large, asymmetrical glass and metal structure which surrounds an auditorium. Through the glass floor of the courtyard, the view is directed into a conference centre and the casino.

The side wings lead in two stages to the ten-storey wing on Behrenstrasse, which is sub-divided by an open space that is as high as the building to form an office zone on the court side and a residential zone on the street side. Facing Behrenstrasse, the building presents a different image which is more typical for Gehry, with closely packed small windows suspended in front of a curving and bulging facade.

Deconstructivism
Frank O. Gehry 1996–99
Mitte, Pariser Platz / Behrenstrasse
▷ S / U Brandenburger Tor, bus 100

Sony Center

Helmut Jahn, who was born in Nürnberg but has lived in Chicago since the 1960s, is regarded as an exponent of precisely the commercial architecture which Frank Gehry's "Deconstructivism" opposes: glass tower blocks, office boxes with maximum profitability, oversized shopping centres. But Jahn would not be so much in demand if he were just a good engineer. His buildings are refreshingly different from the mass of "utility architecture" – assuming one likes his style on principle. Examples are Berlin's narrowest office building at the corner of Kurfürstendamm and Lewishamstrasse and the elegant "Messeturm" (Fair ground tower) in Frankfurt, which at the time was the tallest building in Europe.

Jahn's most important project in Berlin is the Sony Center on Potsdamer Platz, an ensemble dominated by glass and steel and consisting of seven individual buildings. It includes offices, apartments, cinemas, restaurants, a "Filmhaus" and the Sony European headquarters. The central feature in the triangular development is the oval "Forum". The roof construction is a spectacular engineering feat: the outstretched tent roof consists of a length of material fastened to a steel ring which is attached to the neighbouring buildings.

The most striking element is the glass tower block, the tallest building on Potsdamer Platz at 103 metres. It completes the Sony Centre on Potsdamer Platz in that the semi-circular southern facade overlaps the narrower eastern side progressively.

The facade on Bellevuestrasse is also remarkable. The modern residential section is suspended on a steel bridge overhanging the restored neo-baroque facade of the former high class Hotel Esplanade. This was the only partly preserved pre-war building far and wide, and it was not possible to integrate it completely into the new plans, so two rooms which are listed architectural monuments were "translocated".

In 1996 the "Kaisersaal" (Imperial room), which weighs 1300

tonnes, was raised on air cushions in a spectacular feat and shifted by 75 metres. Two walls of the breakfast room remained in their original place, but the ceiling, the floor and the other two walls were cut apart and put together again on the other side of the Esplanade.

The glass Sony Center forms an attractive contrast to the "stone" architecture of the Debis district. But both developments are heavily oriented inwards – the Neue Potsdamer Strasse is more a border between the plots of land than a main urban artery.

A third "neighbourhood" was created in 2001–03 between Potsdamer Platz and Tiergarten. Part of this area is named after the developer, Otto Beisheim, founder of the Metro chain, and is called "Beisheim-Centre". Two high rises, one designed by Hans Kollhoff (Delbrück-Bank) and the other by Hilmer, Sattler & Albrecht (Hotel Ritz-Carlton), dominate the square.

Contemporary Modernism
Helmut Jahn 1996–99
Tiergarten, Potsdamer Platz
www.sonycenter.de
▷ S / U Potsdamer Platz

ARD-Hauptstadtstudio (ARD Studio) and Presse- und Informationsamt der Bundes-regierung (Press and Information Office)

An old proverb claims that Berlin was built from a river boat. But today, the Spree no longer plays an important role in the city, neither as a residential setting nor as a place to stroll. Two new buildings that are close together show the different ways in which an outstanding urban riverside setting can be used.

The ARD television studio (photo) basically completes an existing block. The end building on Wilhelmstrasse corresponds with the neighbouring old building, and on the Spree a lower residential wing provides the link to the adjacent building.

The facade consists of two layers: the outer wall consists of treated prefabricated concrete parts, and the second wall of Meranti wood is visible in narrow recesses next to the windows. The different window designs which considerably soften the massive effect of the block are due to the functional delineation between the individual storeys.

At the centre of the building is a trapezoidal projecting atrium which all office rooms lead into. The glass-covered hall thus becomes the central meeting and communication centre for the editors, a sort of "news exchange for the capital city".

The situation was more complicated for the Press and Information Office, where three old buildings had to be integrated into the complex: the former Reich postal cheque office grouped around several courtyards, a better class slab concrete building on Dorotheenstrasse only completed in 1990 and – at the heart of the plot – the flat structure of a 1970s restaurant with a building volume which dictated the structure of the new building.

The connecting element between the three units is a narrow office wing that was set in front of the fire wall of the postal cheque office. Access is via a corridor in the old building. However, the suspended louver facade with its reflective surface excludes the old building to the rear from the actual building ensemble.

The former seven storey slab concrete building was rendered and painted in a warm orange red, and its ridge roof was replaced by a plain roof. The central building in the ensemble is the low press centre, in which the large room can be sub-divided into up to six smaller units.

Down the river on Santiago Calatrava's elegant Kronprinzen Bridge lies the new Federal Press Conference building by Johanne and Gernot Nalbach. Its facade of small rectangular segments creates an interesting effect, especially when illuminated at night.

Contemporary Modernism
ARD Studio: Laurids and Manfred Ortner with Hans-Peter Wulf 1996–99
Government Press and Information Office: KSP – Engel, Kraemer, Schiedecke and Zimmermann 1996–98 / 2000
Mitte, Reichstagufer, corner of Wilhelmstrasse / corner of Neustädtische Kirchstrasse
▷ S / U Brandenburger Tor, S / U Friedrichstrasse, bus 100

Nordische Botschaften (Nordic Embassies)

The Nordic countries, known for successful design and progressive architecture, are also good for innovation. In the 1990s, when the diplomatic corps moved from Bonn to Berlin, Denmark, Sweden, Norway, Finland and Iceland decided to combine their embassies in a single complex, in order to demonstrate their close relationship within northern Europe while also presenting their individual cultural identities.

The overall plan by Alfred Berger and Tiina Parkkinen was selected from 222 competition entries. The Austrian-Finnish architect duo also designed the shared building where the consulate division and special events rooms are located. But each of the five embassy buildings were planned by architects or architect teams from the respective countries.

The ensemble is connected and shielded from the traffic noise by a curved band of copper that extends as high as the building itself and whose horizontal slats can be tilted at a number of different places. The grounds open on the south side to the quiet Rauchstrasse. The six buildings are assembled around a courtyard with lines of stone marking its alignment.

Through its facade of wood, narrow glass strips and the building-high glass atrium / stairwell, the common building on the right in front is intended to symbolise transparency and openness.

Going counter-clockwise, the Finnish embassy with larch wood venetian blinds placed before its completely glass facade comes first. The both courtyard facades of the Swedish embassy are clearly set off from one another through white limestone on the one and black granite on the other. The building is arranged around a large central room that opens to the intersection of Klingelhöfer- / Stülerstrasse with a large window and a permanently tilted copper slat.

The most striking element of the Norwegian embassy is a 14 metre high block of granite that marks the side facing the courtyard. It symbolises the verticality of the Norwegian landscape. Behind it

lies the entrance to the embassy, with glass exterior walls inspired by the cool clarity of the Norwegian glaciers.

The smallest building, the embassy of Iceland, consists of an office wing enclosed in red natural stone and a separate staircase with connecting rooms.

And finally, the Danish embassy consists of two parts: one follows the soft curve of the copper band, the other carries on the straight line of the courtyard. Between the "soft" wooden part and the sharply cut steel and glass wing, there is a narrow glass atrium, visible from Rauchstrasse.

Contemporary Modernism
Overall plan and common building: Alfred Berger, Tiina Parkkinen;
Finland: Viiva Arkkitehtuuri; Sweden: Wingardh Arkitektkontor; Norway:
Snöhetta; Iceland: Palmar Kristmundsson; Denmark: 3XNielsen 1997–99
Tiergarten, Rauchstrasse
▷ Bus 100, 200

Britische Botschaft (British Embassy)

"You want a Berlin of stone? You get it. You want a 'void facade', rectangular windows, traditional slanted roof? I give it to you. But it is all just scenery." This is what the British Embassy, which was dedicated in 2000, appears to call out to passers-by. Michael Wilford, long-time partner of the famous architect, James Stirling, who died in 1992, created for Berlin on Wilhelmstrasse a post-modern building par excellence. He ironically breaks open the sandstone facade that couldn't be more dull and reveals it to be a mere illusion. The windows rest at an angle behind the "stone wallpaper" and the facade slants toward the neighbouring buildings. In the middle of the street front, where normally a classical palace would have its "Piano Nobile", the most elegant level, this building has a broad, two-storey high gaping hole. Two brightly coloured building elements reach out of the hole towards the passers-by – an absolute stylistic incongruity. The round purple form contains a conference room, the light blue trapezoid is an information centre. The entrance, on the other hand, could not be more simple, smoothly carved into what resembles a courtyard wall.

Wilford's embassy building, which is situated between the elegant "serious" facade of the Hotel Adlon and the light coloured senior citizen's residence by Gustav Peichl and across from the neo-renaissance palace used by the Bundestag, seems to some refreshingly unconventional, to others a desperate call for attention.

The special quality of the new building is found in both interior courtyards around which Wilford grouped the offices for the 120 staff members. The open court of honour set behind the entrance with an English oak tree at its centre leads to a glass covered winter garden, the "communication centre" of the building, whose higher level is reached by climbing a grand stairway and passing by columns. The interior of the building block is dominated by glass, metal cladding on the highest of the six levels and repeated lively colours. They also play a significant role in the first building

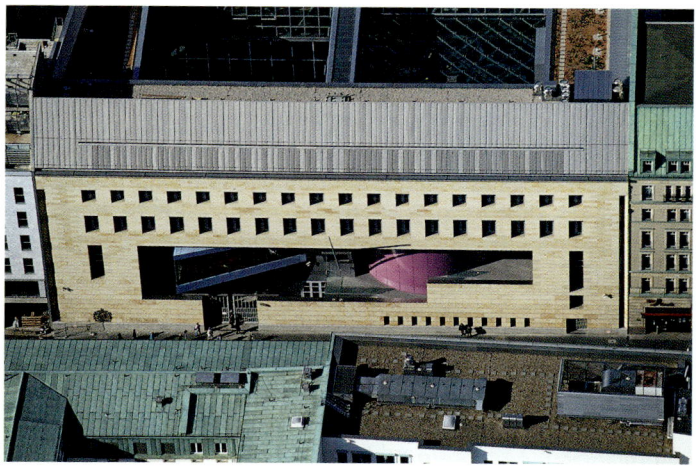

that Wilford designed together with Stirling in Berlin: the "Wissen-schaftszentrum" on the Landwehr Canal – a conspicuous pink-blue striped building located diagonally behind the New National Gallery.

Geographically, the United Kingdom is adding to an old tradition: On this very site from 1884 to the Second World War, His Majesty's Ambassador resided in what was once the palace of the railway entrepreneur, Strousberg. The new building, which incidentally is the first embassy building world-wide to have been built completely with private funds and only rented by the British state, is designed to meet the evolving demands of diplomatic representation: the interior with its successful room sequence for receptions and special events and the exterior, a facade that seeks to balance English understatement with the freshness of popular culture.

Post-modernism
Michael Wilford 1998–2000
Mitte, Wilhelmstrasse 70 / 71
▷ S / U Brandenburger Tor, bus 100, 200

Neues Kranzler-Eck (New Kranzler-Eck)

The glass wall tower extends sixty metres high behind the time-honoured Kranzler-Eck. Its razor sharp point juts out almost into the avenue of Kurfürstendamm. There is no doubt that the star architect Helmut Jahn provided the City-West with a new attraction, pepping up a shopping district which had had difficulty competing with the new old Mitte district after re-unification.

In addition to the Kranzler-Eck with its characteristic rotunda, the 1950s building ensemble also includes the former Bilka department store – now a Karstadt Sport store – with a facade decorated with diamond-shaped elements. The 16 storey high-rise extends across the entire lot up to the city rail viaduct. To the west between the high-rise, the Victoria building from 1963 and another new nine storey building, there is a shopping arcade running from Kudamm to Kantstrasse. On the other side, the new and old Kranzler-Eck form an intimate inner courtyard from which during the day the sounds of parakeets, peasants and ducks seeps in through two large aviaries. Between the arcade and courtyard there is an impressive seven storey passageway.

The entire building complex makes a powerful impression. Glass walls set in front and side wings are effective in blurring the structure of the glass giant. On both sides of the 16 storey tower that protrudes outward to an empty point facing the Kudamm stand buildings half its size, one of which hovers over the Bilka department store. The top of the building next door recalls the jagged crowned roofs of expressionist buildings designed in the twenties and, like the glass roof that only partially protects the arcade from wind and weather, serves very little function. Even worse is the Déjà-vu-sensation that the New Kranzler-Eck inspires in Berliners. The Kudamm building seems much like a copy of the Sony Center at Potsdamer Platz. One has to look carefully to recognise the distinct differences hidden in the details of the facade design.

But Jahn can create works of a very different nature, as can be seen by taking a short detour along the Kudamm to Adenauer-platz. In 1992–94 the most narrow office building in Berlin was created on a corner lot only 2.5 metres wide.

Directly across from the New Kranzler-Eck the New Kudamm-Eck greets passers-by with a grey heaviness. This curving building, which replaced the 1970s Kudamm-Eck that was torn down in 1998, is the work of the ubiquitous Hamburg office gmp von Gerkan, Marg & Partner. Another high rise was built in 2005: the Hotel Concorde, designed by Jan Kleihues, son of IBA director, Josef Paul Kleihues.

Contemporary Modernism
Helmut Jahn 1998–2000
Charlottenburg, Kurfürstendamm / Joachimsthaler Strasse
▷ U Kurfürstendamm, bus M19, M29

Landesvertretungen
(State Representative Offices)

The state representative offices, with which the German states are represented in Berlin, are as impressive as many of the embassies representing independent nations. Bavaria, Hamburg, Saxony and Saxony-Anhalt reside in prestigious pre-war buildings (the curious office representing Berlin in Germany no longer exists). Many of the other federal states had elaborate new buildings erected. Five buildings for seven federal states were constructed on the grounds of the former Ministers' Gardens, just north of Potsdamer Platz. This used to be where the extensive garden of the Foreign Office had been. After World War Two the area remained fallow, caught within the prohibited zone of the Berlin Wall.

The buildings constructed between 1998 and 2001 are oriented towards classical modernism. Only the Hesse office strikes a tone pleasantly different from the elegant reserve radiating from the other buildings. It is particularly interesting to compare the different facade structures.

The representative offices of Lower Saxony and Schleswig-Holstein are combined in a single block on the north side of the street. A broad glass atrium with an external steel construction is situated between the two parallel rectangular building blocks. The grey limestone facade is enlivened by the irregularly set windows and the red metal profiles which mark the top of each level. Between the windows the facade panels have varying widths and lengths and between each metal profile lies a single row of panels.

The Rhineland-Pfalz office faces the street as a simple cube, in which the entrance and roof area are not included. The horizontal window formats are characteristic. The light-coloured natural stone plates are also set in various widths.

The Saarland office is built with elegant proportions. The simple cube form expands into an open grid in back. Here the back wall is dominated by squares and rectangles – in the large glass areas of

the three middle axes and in the smaller windows. The facade stones have been selected and positioned evenly.

Two J-shaped building blocks connected by a glass atrium form the joint offices of Brandenburg and Mecklenburg-Vorpommern. The black slate plates are set vertically between the groupings of three windows and lie horizontally at the ceiling level of each storey.

And finally, the Hesse office building is varied in shape and form with characteristic overhanging storeys (photo). The sandstone facade opens on three sides to continuous bands of windows. Only the east side displays a narrow window format.

Contemporary Modernism
Lower Saxony / Schleswig-Holstein: Cornelsen & Seelinger, Seelinger & Vogels; Rhineland-Pfalz: Heinle, Wischer and Partner; Saarland: Peter Alt & Thomas Britz; Brandenburg / Mecklenburg-Vorpommern: gmp von Gerkan, Marg & Partner; Hesse: Michael Christl, Joachim Bruchhäuser; 1998–2001
Mitte, In den Ministergärten
▷ S / U Potsdamer Platz, bus 123, 148, 200

Bundeskanzleramt (Federal Chancellery), Paul-Löbe- und Marie-Elisabeth-Lüders-Haus (Löbe and Lüders Building)

The "ribbon of government buildings" stretches like a band across the meander of the Spree to the north of the Reichstag. From west to east it includes the "Chancellor's garden", the Federal Chancellery (photo), the Paul Löbe building with offices for parliamentarians and the Marie Elisabeth Lüders building, which also contains the parliamentary library.

The master plan by the Berlin architects Axel Schultes and Charlotte Frank has been celebrated as a stroke of genius. No other proposal envisaged such a radical re-structuring of the meander of the Spree, where the earlier buildings of the Alsen Quarter, with the exception of the Swiss embassy, were destroyed in the war. It is symbolic that the Chancellery, as the centre of government, does not compete architecturally with the seat of parliament.

The one building that was left unrealised in order to save money just happens to be the one building intended for the public. In the master plan it is referred to simply as the "Forum" between the Chancellery and the Löbe building. This is why the "ribbon" is interrupted at its centre: The Chancellery stands alone in the landscape like a large concrete sculpture.

Between and above the two five-storey administrative wings rises the 36 metre high "main building" containing the offices of the Chancellor and his ministers of state, the cabinet room and conference rooms.

To the north and south respectively, a large arch is cut into the plain wall, to the east (to the main entrance) and west the outer walls are broken down into various concrete and glass layers. This gives the building an extraordinary transparency and lightness. Both sides wings, with ground plans resembling a comb, convey a very different impression. The office space is grouped around completely glass-covered courtyards. This makes the long side walls that alternate between windowless concrete and large glass areas

appear compact and fortress-like. The Löbe building, designed by the Munich architect Stephan Braunfels, appears both monumental and yet more delicate. It is connected to the Chancellery and Lüders building by far-extending roofs resting on narrow concrete pillars. Along both sides of an atrium that extends along the entire length of the building, the offices are again arranged like a comb – but here they extend deeper. The covered courtyards remain open, integrated through a roof structure that runs continuously throughout the entire building. The conference rooms are situated in rounded glass wings.

North of the Löbe building stands a blue day-care centre for children of the Bundestag staff that was designed by the Viennese architect Gustav Peichl.

Contemporary Modernism
Overall plan and Federal Chancellery: Axel Schultes with Charlotte Frank 1997–2001; Paul Löbe building and Marie Elisabeth Lüders building: Stephan Braunfels 1997–2002
Tiergarten
▷ U Bundestag, bus 100

Pei-Bau – Schauhaus des Deutschen Historischen Museums Berlin (Schauhaus of the German Historical Museum in Berlin)

I. M. Pei is usually an architect of large projects. Born in 1917 in Canton, China, he came to the United States in 1935 to study and ended up staying there until today. He studied with Walter Gropius at Harvard, was for decades in charge of one of the largest architecture firms in the world and since the 1960s was responsible for a number of spectacular construction projects: the John F. Kennedy Library in Boston, the East Wing of the National Gallery of Art across from the Capitol building in Washington, the Bank of China Tower in Hong Kong. He joined the architectural elite, however, in the 1980s with his reconstruction of the Louvre in Paris, which culminates with the installation of a glass pyramid in the honour court of the venerable king's palace.

Pei felt connected to modernism his entire life – even when most of his American colleagues were seeking salvation in post-modernism. It is his museum designs that stand out amongst his immense oeuvre.

Pei was presented with the task of creating a building for temporary exhibitions on the thankless plot of ground behind the Baroque Zeughaus that could hold its own without outdoing the older buildings in the area. The basic form of the three-storey building is a triangle with a slightly protruding wall on the southwest side facing the Zeughaus. Pei concentrated the exhibition rooms in a central building structure clad in natural stone, which from the outside appears block-like and inaccessible. To the southwest and east it is enveloped by an additional structure made of glass and framed by steel.

The foyer consists of more than merely the curved glass wing: it also strides outward into the massive building structure and a second smaller building section on the east side. The pillars and supports, false ceilings, galleries and a single large round window are so skilfully integrated into the space that the final impression

is of a complex room of various shapes. Visitors can wander through the foyer in different directions. The effect of light and shadows and the many changing perspectives draws curious visitors into the exhibition rooms on the various levels. There is also a careful attention to detail that is quite impressive.

With this relatively small, prominently-situated exhibition building, I.M. Pei secured himself a lifelong seat of honour among the architects of the most successful building creations in Berlin.

Two new cultural institutions situated behind the Pei building are also worthy of a visit: the Centrum Hungaricum, built in 2006 / 07 and designed by the Hamburg star architect Peter Schweger, and the gallery 'Am Kupfergraben 10' with their bare, whitewashed brick walls (David Chipperfield 2003–07).

Contemporary Modernism
I.M. Pei 1998–2003
Mitte, Hinter dem Gießhaus
Open: daily 10–18 hrs., Tel. 20 30 44 44
www.dhm.de
▷ S / U Friedrichstrasse, bus 100

Akademie der Künste (Academy of Arts) and Hotel Adlon

The two buildings that caused the greatest architectural debates in recent years stand side by side on Pariser Platz: Here the Hotel Adlon, whose conservative style was seen as a herald of a new traditionalism in architecture. There the glass front of the Academy of Arts, which stood diametrically opposed to the design regulations for the development of the plaza and was only realised thanks to special permission granted by the building senator.

Both buildings show two different, yet typical ways of dealing with the past. In the 1950s the war ruins were completely torn down, with one exception: the studio and exhibition wing of the Prussian Academy of Arts, built in 1905 / 06 according to plans by Ernst von Ihnes. In 1937 general building inspector Albert Speer worked here on his models for the design of a "world capital" called Germania; later selected artists and members of the East German Academy were invited to set up their studios here.

After the design by the office of Günter Behnisch was unanimously selected by the plenum of the re-unified Academy of Arts in 1994, the historical halls in the centre of the property were preserved. The first, now named the Max Liebermann Hall, was maintained in its ruinous condition, the four other rooms were restored to their original state. Behnisch, who was also the architect of the Munich Olympic Stadium and the glass Bundestag in Bonn, and his partners surrounded the pre-war building with an airy new building made of glass and steel, exposed concrete and wood, providing lots of space for visitors to saunter (in the right part of the photograph). The offices are concentrated in a narrow wing along the firewall to the neighbouring building.

Although the glass facade, which blurs the individual levels of the building structure, seems unspectacular, the interior of the building surprises with its sloping floors and slanted window frames that press against each other and support and are interwoven into one another; with bridges and galleries that extend through the

entire high-ceilinged foyer; with the play of long perspectives and intimate islands of calm.

The new building of Hotel Adlon (in the left part of the photograph), in contrast, conjures a history through an architecture that on first glance appears old. With an external sandstone facade of varying degrees of brightness, the simplified historical decorative forms and the slanted roof clad with oxidised copper sheeting, the new building by the Berlin office of Patzschke and Klotz recalls its historical model from 1907. The older building, however, was only half as wide (the corner of Wilhelmstrasse had been occupied by another building), and although the same height, contained one less storey.

Contemporary Modernism (Academy of Arts) / Neo-historicism (Hotel Adlon)
Academy of Arts: Günter Behnisch with Werner Durth 1999–2005;
Hotel Adlon: Rüdiger Patzschke, Rainer-Michael Klotz 1995–97
Mitte, Pariser Platz 4
Open: Tues–Sun 11–20 Uhr, Tel. 200 57 10 00
www.adk.de
▷ S / U Brandenburger Tor, bus 100

Hauptbahnhof (Central Train Station)

While in great cities, such as Paris and London, there are still terminus stations in which railroad lines from various directions end,
since May 2006 Berlin has only had one "Central Train Station."
Eight terminus train stations were built in Berlin between 1838 and
1875; however, since 1882 a city railway has run east and west
through the metropolis. After German reunification, the so-called
"mushroom concept" was approved and executed in a modified
form by 2006: The majority of rail traffic passes through a 3.5-kilo-
metre-long north-south tunnel and is then redirected in the north
via a circular railway – representing the stem and top of the "mushroom." The city railway forms the "mushroom's brim," and at the
crossing point of tunnel and city railway, the new central train
station was built. The winning design was created by gmp von
Gerkan, Marg & Partner.

Located 15 metres below street level are 4 railroad platforms for
the north-south railway; 6 platforms for east-west connections
are located 10 metres above street level. These are supported by
four 680-metre-long bridge constructions that span the Humbolt
Harbor. The upper train platforms are covered by a basket arch
shaped steel and glass construction, which is up to 17 metres high
and 68 metres wide.

Situated perpendicular to this roof, and marking the tunnel's
course, is the 210-metre-long and 43-metre-wide north-south
roof under which lies the actual train station hall – with three open
connecting- and shop levels. This room is supported by two
gantry-type structures, which span the east-west roof. The construction of these two bridges was spectacular. First they were
mounted – in four halves – onto the corner buildings, then, like draw-
bridges – each weighing 1250 tons – they were lowered at a rate of
six metres per hour and connected to each other with a clearance
of just two centimetres.

The fact that the external design of the train station was not

based exclusively on its structure was evident in the 2007 hurricane, when a 1.35 ton horizontal brace fell from one of the tower structures. In fact, only the vertical supports are structurally necessary: The horizontal elements are purely decorative and are hung in place, although they have now been secured.

The Deutsche Bahn AG's decision to install an unimpressive flat ceiling on the lower platform area, rather than the airy vaulted one designed by the architects, resulted in a court battle, which architect Meinhard von Gerkan initially won; the battle, however, wages on. The Deutsche Bahn AG also ignored the results of a public survey conducted in 2002, which showed that the majority of those asked wanted the new train station to be called "Lehrter Bahnhof" – after the original station that had once stood on this spot but that was destroyed during the Second World War.

Contemporary Modernism
Meinhard von Gerkan, Jürgen Hillmer for gmp von Gerkan, Marg & Partner 1996–2006
Tiergarten (Moabit), Europaplatz
▷ S / U Hauptbahnhof

Mexikanische Botschaft / Diplomatenviertel (Mexican Embassy / Diplomatic Quarter)

In front of the Leipziger Gate, in the early 19th century, a neigh-bourhood developed where anyone who wanted to get away from the hustle and bustle of the city, and who could afford to live in a villa or at least an apartment in a stately city building with a back and front garden, could do so.

The proximity to the government quarter on and around Wil-helmstrasse soon turned the area into one of the favourite places for foreign diplomats to live. In 1938 alone, 37 – almost three quar-ters of all embassies and legations in Berlin – were built on the small strip of land situated between the Tiergarten and Landwehr-kanal that was commonly referred to as the "diplomatic quarter". In 1938 Albert Speer began to design several new embassies for "friendly" or occupied countries, such as Italy, Japan, Spain and Norway. These buildings survived the war, as did the former guest house of the Krupp Company that is now home to the Canisius-Kolleg (Tiergartenstrasse). The majority of the older buildings, how-ever, fell victim to the bombs. For decades the area was dominated by a cityscape of wastelands and ruins, but since the 1990s the quarter has been rebuilt bit by bit. As early as 1987 an impressive urban villa project was built on Rauchstrasse as part of the Inter-national Building Exhibition (director: Rob Krier, with contributions by various architects 1983 / 84), and Berlin's only two green build-ings are located between Rauch- and Corneliusstrasse (coordina-tion: Frei Otto and Hermann Kendel 1988–90).

Located next to one another on Klingelhöferstrasse is the most conspicuous collection of buildings in the reconstructed diplo-matic quarter – the Nordic Embassies –, and the building with the unusual façade, the Mexican Embassy (photo). From a concrete frame, the Mexican architects Teodoro Gonzalez de Leon and Fran-cisco Serrano hung a "curtain wall" consisting of 18 metre high inclined concrete pillars, that slants to the side. A second row of pillars slants backwards and between these two sets of pillars, the

entrance opens up into the central rotunda, the form of which is visible on the outside through the cylindrical roof structure – a motif reminiscent of Le Corbusier. The striking white colour of the concrete facade comes from the addition of marble chips and marble powder to the concrete.

Other noteworthy buildings include the CDU National Headquarters (Petzinka Pink) and the Academy of the Konrad Adenauer Foundation (Thomas van den Valentyn), the Austrian Embassy (Hans Hollein 1999 / 2000) and the Indian Embassy (Léon Wohlhage Wernik 1999–2001), as well as the representations of the states of North Rhein-Westphalia (Petzinka Pink) and Bremen (Léon Wohlhage Wernik). Under construction since 2009 on Clara-Wieck-Strasse is the "diplomatic park" with twelve city villas, classical-styled apartment buildings with luxurious apartments.

Contemporary Modernism
Mexican Embassy: Teodoro Gonzalez de Leon and Francisco Serrano
1999–2001
Tiergarten, Klingelhöferstrasse 3
▷ Bus 200

Mediaspree

"Mediaspree" is the name of the project with which the state of Berlin hopes to gentrify the riverbank to the southwest of the old city centre. This four-kilometre stretch of the Spree bank situated between the Jannowitz and Elsen Bridges has been primarily used for commercial purposes for centuries. After World War Two, part of this stretch of the Spree served as the border between East and West Berlin. In the 1990s urban planners set their sights on the area and in 2002 a land utilization plan was passed whose framework was determined not by projects by one main developer but rather by several individual ones. Vigorous resistance arose against these developers because by then an underground culture with discotheques, clubs and beach bars along the riverbank had developed and the proponents of this culture fought against the investors' plans under the banner, "Sink the Media Spree." Nonetheless, it seems that, sooner or later, the entire riverbank will be developed. It is worth strolling along the Spree, even though the planned river promenade is only partially finished.

Most of the impressive buildings are located on the river's right bank. These include – looking from Jannowitz Bridge – the 13-storey high office tower "Trias" (Lucia Beringer and Gunther Wawrik 1992–96, today the BVG headquarters), Radialsystem V (a former wastewater pumping station that was expanded with a new structure 2004–06 designed by Gerhard Spangenberg and transformed into an event venue) and the Energieforum, which the Hamburg architects Bothe, Richter and Teherani expanded with a new building that surrounds the site's old industrial structure (2000–02). A tunnel at the entrance leads straight through the old structure and into a high glass atrium. Berlin's largest multifunctional hall, O_2 World, is uninteresting architecturally. Opened in 2008, its developers have tellingly not revealed the names of its architects. Concerts, ice hockey games of the "Eisbären" (Berlin's hockey

team) and basketball games of "Alba" (Berlin's basketball team) can host up to 17000 spectators here.

The East Harbor was built in 1907–13 behind the Neo-Gothic Oberbaum Bridge. In 2000 the old warehouses along the quay wall were converted into office space: The 1928 / 29 "egg cooling house" was converted into Universal Music's German headquarters, and the former Warehouse West now houses the television station, MTV Deutschland. Warehouse East is now used by fashion companies, as is the new office building on the Elsen Bridge, "Labels 2" (photo), with its striking green concrete facade (2008/09 by the Basel architects HFF). Another conversion is the "Design-hotel" – part of the Spanish NH Hotel Group – with its spectacular projecting "Kranhaus" (Sergei Tchoban 2008–10) facing the river. The office complex "Treptowers" was constructed in 1995–98; it includes the 125-metre-high Allianz Tower (by Gerhard Spangenberg) and the 60-metre-high "Twin Towers" (Kieferle & Partner).

Contemporary Modernism
Mitte / Friedrichshain / Kreuzberg, since the 1990s
▷ S Ostbahnhof

Niederländische Botschaft (Dutch Embassy)

The Dutch builders fell for the site – a corner lot on the old harbour with a view of the Friedrich Canal – originally built by the Dutch – and wanted their embassy to be an architectural exclamation point, an open, solitary building. Building regulations dictated a perimeter block structure to the eave height, which was also to contain apartments. An unsolvable problem? Not for Rem Koolhaas, one of the most innovative and daring architects of the last decades and head of the Rotterdam Office for Metropolitan Architecture (OMA). He had had a score to settle with Berlin since the 1990s, when he infuriated the jury of the Potsdamer Platz competition, because he did not wish to share their "petty bourgeois, old-fashioned, reactionary and amateurish image of the city." And he settled the score in an unusual way when his competition-winning design for the Dutch embassy was built 2000–04.

On the corner of the site he built a glass and aluminium faced 27-metre-long cube – precisely the prescribed eave height. On the rear edge of the property, as a connection to the neighbouring buildings, he placed an L-shaped narrow structure, from the walls of which close-meshed grid plates are suspended like a veil. The services equipment is located in this building, as well as three official residencies and guest apartments. An asphalt ramp leads from the Klosterstrasse between the cube and the L-shaped building to the elevated courtyard, where the main entrance is located.

Not only are the grounds and facades unusual, but the interior of the cube completely breaks with all common ideas of what a building should be. It is not divided up into conventional floors; rather the various rooms are offset from each other over a total of twelve floors, which are connected via a "traject," an almost 200-metre-long corridor made up of ramps and stairs that twists through the entire building up to the roof garden. The ambassador's apartment, a fitness studio, which is open to all employ-

ees, and a cafeteria are all located on the upper floors of the cube. Most of the interior walls are made out of exposed concrete, and a few are faced in wood. The projecting dark "skybox" on the west side is part of the conference room.

Contemporary Modernism
Rem Koolhaas / OMA 2000–04
Mitte, Klosterstrasse 50
▷ U Klosterstrasse

Townhouses (on the Friedrichswerder)

For a few years now inner city living in Berlin, too, has no longer been limited to flats in tenement structures or new buildings that fill gaps left by the war. In 1996 planning began for a small but outstanding and extremely unusual neighbourhood in the best location: the "townhouses" on the Friedrichswerder. Long ago, during the Baroque period and Berlin's first city expansion, apartments and stores stood next to each other on small streets here. Following the destruction of the area during the Second World War, East German urban planners levelled everything between the office district of the Friedrichstadt quarter and the building block that served as the SED's headquarters – today the Foreign Office – creating a wide stretch of grass.

As entire blocks disappeared between uniform office building facades following German reunification, city planners designed a small-scaled, architecturally diverse island for this area where private developers were to build individual townhouses in which residents could work and live.

Two blocks were divided up into forty-seven 125 and 280 square metre building lots, each 4.50 to 9.75 metres wide and 13 to 16 metres deep. The houses were supposed to be at least four, a maximum of five stories high, and one- or two-storey additions were permitted on half of each lot. Each house has a back yard. The ability to live and work under a single roof was the specific goal, and the area's living quality was guaranteed by limiting the use of commercially used square footage.

In 2003 the State of Berlin presented the townhouse project and within a week all forty-seven plots had been reserved. The prices for the lots were much lower than they would have been on the free market: between 120 000 and 340 000 Euros; a house, including its plot, was to cost no more than a million Euros.

In order to guarantee the architectural standard, the state-run development association hired five architects, "to test the feasi-

bility and liveability of narrow, high houses." Bernd Albers, Johanne and Gernot Nalbach, Theo Brenner, Behles & Jochimsen and Abcarius & Burns each designed two prototype houses that varied greatly in floor plan, facade design, materials and overall character. A common feature shared by all, however, was the varied forms of their street and garden facades. Based on these model designs, the owners hired their own architects to design their houses. In order to prevent the houses from becoming objects of speculation, all owners had to agree not to sell their homes for ten years.

On the block just north of this, the 'Foreign Office Quarter' was built in 2007–10; it includes five buildings, designed by different architects, with offices, apartments and a hotel.

Contemporary Modernism
Approximately 30 different architects 2004–10
Mitte, between Jägerstrasse, Kurstrasse, Alte Leipziger Strasse and
Nieder- / Oberwallstrasse
▷ Bus 100

Jacob-und-Wilhelm-Grimm-Zentrum Berlin (Jacob and Wilhelm Grimm Center Berlin)

Books belong to yesterday – the future lies in the Internet and e-books, or so they say. But we are not there yet, and so Humboldt University was given – at the book age's alleged end – a new and prestigious library. The building impresses with its clarity, but takes the breath away from its more playful users. The design by the Berlin-based Swiss architect Max Dudler is characterized, in fact, by an almost merciless right-angled severity.

Twelve branch libraries and the main library, which until now had been housed in the back of the State Library, are united here, creating Germany's largest cohesive open access library stock – nearly a million and a half books. When designing the library, use was made of past experiences. Situated in the centre of the building, parallel to its south facade, is the main reading hall, which has a stepped structure, extends over five stories and is flooded with light, thanks to its glass roof. Its 250 work spaces are arranged over nine terraces, so that one's gaze may wander but through traffic is avoided. Individual carrels are located on the narrow sides and in group areas; the open shelf libraries are located along the building's sides. The floors and the individual areas are sometimes separated from one another by glass elements, so that visitors can work in the direct vicinity of the books they need. The 1,250 work and reading spaces are located throughout the building on its seven floors and in the parent-child area and children's library located over the roofs of the city.

Because of the sheer quantity of the book stock it is only in the reading hall and the foyer that share the expansiveness of Scharoun's State Library. Otherwise the building is characterized by a sense of concentrated tightness, a feeling that is intensified by the fact that the entire building, down to the chairs and tables is based on a grid with the dimensions of book shelves.

What awaits the visitor is already visible in the facades, with their seemingly endless rows of narrow and high rectangular win-

dows in a marble-faced wall grid. The monotony is broken up only
by the variation of the three window formats, behind which are the
magazine, reading areas and special areas. While the lower building elements act as a visual bridge to the neighbouring buildings,
the south facade with the main entrance rises straight up and high
above Berlin's eave height.

It is, however, this formal clarity that lends the Grimm Centre its
unusual quality. The building and the interior furnishings are characterized by exceptional attention to detail and the tasteful choice
of materials. The floors are covered with either Jura Stone or black
linoleum, the walls and ceilings are painted white, and the built-in
shelves and walls in the reading hall are made of red cherry wood.

Contemporary Modernism
Max Dudler 2005–09
Mitte, Geschwister-Scholl-Strasse 3
www.grimm-zentrum.hu-berlin.de
▷ S / U Friedrichstrasse

Glossary

Apse (plural apses): semicircular vaulted recess, in church architecture often used as the end of the chancel, a side chancel or alter niche.

Architrave: the lowest part of an entablature.

Attic: a low storey above the upper cornice of a building.

Choir: the liturgically and often architecturally most important architectural element of a church, usually located in the eastern part of the church. In contrast to the common area, the choir – in more elaborate structures the inner area, the inner choir – was reserved for the clerics.

Doric column: the oldest column form without a base and with a plain capital. The column is made up of rounded segments (drums), tapers toward the top (swelling slightly outward at the base) and is subdivided in parallel channels (flutes). The Doric entablature consists of a plain architrave, a so-called triglyph-metope frieze (partially decorated with a relief-like structure), and a crown cornice, usually decorated with palmettes.

Pinnacle: a Gothic ornamental structure used, above all, on towers and buttresses – a small tower made of a four-sided base and a pointed crown.

Ionic column: slender, fluted column with a base and voluted capitals (formed by paired scrolling volutes). The architrave is made up of three separate layers (originally beams); the frieze is smooth and partially decorated with reliefs. Often referred to as the 'feminine order' and used for fine art buildings.

Bay: rectangular or square subunit of, above all, Gothic rooms created by a vaulted ceiling and four columns.

Capital: upper, often elaborately decorated final element of a supporting element (pillar, column, engaged column), transition to vault or the suspended horizontal building element (entablature, architrave).

Colossal Structure: columns or pilasters that span more than one, usually two, storeys (colossal pillar or columns).

Corinthian column: at first sight very similar to the Ionic order, nonetheless with very different capitals consisting of acanthus leaves.

Nave: lengthwise in direction, the part of the church that was open to the public, in contrast to the transept and the choir; it has one or more aisles.

Lantern: the top, usually open, tower-like superstructure on a dome.

Pilaster strip: flat narrow wall strip applied to the wall surface as a vertical organizational element.

Mansard roof: a special form of the saddle roof used, above all, in the Baroque period; the ridged roof has two slopes on either side, the lower slope having the steeper pitch and it is under this part that the attic rooms were built.

Pilaster: furnished with a base and capital, slender wall attachments in contrast to plain pilaster strips.

Polygon: a structure with three or more sides, for instance the outer wall of a choir – with several openings – in medieval churches (choir polygon).

Portico: in front of a building, a covered ambulatory supported by columns or pillars.

Risalit (Projection): a part of the building that usually juts out in the roof area in the middle or on the sides of a façade (middle or corner risalit).

Rustication: ashlar masonry, often imitated with grooves in plaster.

Column: round support with a classic form with base and capital, in contrast to a pillar.

Column orders: developed by the Greeks (Doric, Ionic, Corinthian), the Romans expanded the classical orders (Tuscan, Composite); columns end in an entablature, which is divided into three parts: architrave, frieze and cornice. Main orders: Doric, Ionic, Corinthian.

Bow: in church architecture – an arch supported by two free-standing pillars that separates two naves from each other.

Tambour: a wall that supports a dome.

Eaves-fronted house: a house, the longer side (eave) of which faces the street, in contrast to one whose shorter side (gable) faces the street.

Trophies: ancient decorations with arms, flags, etc. used on buildings, a practice taken up again in the Renaissance.

Crossing: in ecclesiastic structures, the place in a cruciform church where the transept crosses the nave; leads from the congregation area to the choir.

Index of Buildings

Index of Persons